HERSTORY
A SPIRITUAL JOURNEY

A WINDOW INTO MULTICULTURAL AUSTRALIA
STORIES AND RECIPES

WOMENS FEDERATION FOR WORLD PEACE AUSTRALIA

WFWP Australia Head Office

42-46 Bartley Rd,
Belgrave Heights, VIC 3160

Copyright © 2019 WFWP Australia
Melbourne, Sydney, Brisbane.
All rights reserved, including the right to reproduce this book or portions thereof in any form whatsoever. For information, contact WFWP Australia.

Website: www.wfwpaustralia.org
E-mail: contact@wfwpaustralia.org
Facebook: www.facebook.com/wfwpoceania
Youtube: Women's Federation for World Peace, Oceania

HerStory Editorial Team
Editor In Chief: Anne Bellavance
Proof Reader: Sara Cohen
Design: Antoine Bellavance, Giulia Iacono, Vishwa Thurairajah
Book Cover: Antoine Bellavance

About Us

Empowering Women
Strengthening Families
Connecting Communities

WFWP Chapters adhere to the principle that women working together, taking initiative and empowering one another across traditional lines of race, culture and religion to create healthy families are resolving the complex problems of our societies and world.
Ultimately, solutions come when true partnerships between men and women are established in all levels of society. The beginning point is within society's most elemental level - the family.

Vision: Women working together to realise one global family rooted in a culture of sustainable peace.

Mission: Empowering women as peacebuilders and leaders in the family to transform the community, nation and world. Through education, advocacy, partnership, reconciliation and humanitarian service, WFWPI aims to create an environment of peace and wellbeing for future generations and people of all races, cultures and religious creeds.

Women from WFWP are committed to:
- *Serving communities* - humanitarian projects within Australia and the Pacific Islands.
- *Strengthening the family* - workshops, forums, seminars and conferences.
- *Reconciling differences and healing wounds of the past* - Bridge of Peace ceremonies.
- *Global Women's Peace Network (GWPN)* - The Global Women's Peace Network (GWPN) brings together leaders, organisations and governments to solve pressing social issues and to secure an environment for equitable human development. Through peace leadership based on the feminine aspect of human nature, GWPN seeks to ensure lasting peace and prosperity for generations to come.

Since the inauguration of WFWP International in 1992, WFWP is active in 122 nations worldwide. As an NGO, WFWP obtained the prestigious General Consultative Status with the Economic and Social Council of the United Nations after five years of International humanitarian service.

WFWP Australia supports projects within Australia and the Island Nations of the Oceania region. These include: Global Women's Peace Network; Speech Contest; Workshops on topical issues; Seminars, Conferences and Forums on Peace Building; Reconciliation through the Bridge of Peace ceremonies; Annual Walk-a-thon to support our Projects in the Pacific Islands; Books for the Islands; New Hope Academy School in the Solomon Islands; Pacific Island's Scholarship Fund; Endeavour Credit; Women's Sewing Centres; and, Island Lights Project.

Join us in our efforts to promote a culture of peace through: fostering dialogue, developing projects that nurture reconciliation and conflict resolution, supporting projects that serve the community and overcome racial boundaries; all centering on the inherent feminine characteristics of care, empathy, support, nurturing and cooperation. Connect with other likeminded people around the world who are dedicated to a more harmonious and peaceful world.

Check out our Australia website to see where you can get involved:
www.wfwpaustralia.org

Foreword

Her Story is a compilation of inspirational and heart-felt stories of women who shared their journey during the Women's Federation for World Peace Australia Her Story sessions in Melbourne, Victoria. Entwined throughout our lives are our values and spirituality; it is this deeper journey that Her Story reveals. Our life journey is a collection of choices and decisions that are made based on our values, our passions and what we hold to be true for ourselves and our family. Trials, challenges and crossroads in our lives require big choices and decisions. It is our hope that Her Story will be a guiding light, a moral compass and a source of strength when you are faced with decisions that affect yourself and those you love.

The Her Story collection is our history, our heart, our spirituality, our love and our culture as one human family. The collection represents a window into multi-cultural Australia. The women featured in Her Story come from all 'walks of life'; they express their unique cultural, religious and ethnic backgrounds.

A significant part of our culture is what we love to cook and share around the dinner table. The second part of HerStory is a collection of each woman's favourite recipe as Starters, Mains or Sweets. The recipes are as diverse as multi-cultural Australia. We hope that you enjoy exploring them and sourcing out the ingredients in all the wonderful multi-cultural food stores located in your neighbourhood's.

Acknowledgements

Naturally, the first person to thank is the founder of WFWP International, Dr. Hak Ja Han Moon, who is the inspiration behind Her Story. She has worked on the global arena to develop a culture of peace for over fifty years with her husband, the late Rev. Dr. Sun Myung Moon. Hak Ja Han Moon's heart has always been to empower and liberate women, hence the founding of WFWPI in 1992.

On behalf of our Australian WFWP Chapters, I would like to acknowledge all our members and volunteers who give with a mother's heart in serving their families and communities to bind us closer together in harmony and forgiveness as one human family. This is such a profound job description, the most important job of all. Without stable, safe and connected individuals, families and communities, our society would be on a train track to disaster. Our mother's give hope; thank you my sisters for your beautiful hearts.

I would also like to acknowledge all the men in our lives for their support and kindness; especially our partners and sons. Together we make a whole and together we can bring real change in the lives of each other, our families and communities. Your patience and love is deeply appreciated.

To all the ladies who shared their courageous and heartfelt stories, I know your story offers a guiding light to those who are on a similar journey. You are an inspiration and a testament of 'living for the sake of others.' Your persistence and determination to build a better world for your families is the driving force behind building a culture of peace with sound values. Thank you for sharing your wisdom with us.

Anne Bellavance
Vice-president, WFWP International (Oceania region)
President, WFWP Australia

CONTENTS

Starters

Ingrid Hindell – From Catholic to eclectic ... 1
    Far-east Hommus ... 4

Miti Tangianau – A travelling journey ... 5
    Seaweed Soup A La Miti ... 8

Jacinta Darbishire – A rebellious spirit ... 9
    Spring Kimchi Salad ... 17

Lucy Verstegen – Beautiful Music ... 18
    Gourmet open Sandwiches with Cheese ... 23

Main Dishes

Monica Zaman – Dreams in her eyes ... 24
    Spiced Flatbread (Methi paratha) ... 32
    Almond Stuffed Meatballs with spicy tomato sauce ... 33

Naya (Barbara) Vondracek - A first generation Aussie ... 35
    Naya's Hungarian Chicken ... 46

Zakia Baig – The unheard Story ... 47
    Chicken or Lamb Biryani - from Khana Khazana ... 52

Jenny Funston – Journey to Japan ... 54
    Crunchy Tuna Surprise ... 62

Noriko Jede – White Butterfly ... 63
    Sushi – A traditional Japanese dish ... 68
    Tempura – A traditional Japanese dish ... 69

Patricia Bekc Mayele – From Congo to Australia ... 70
    Ceebu Jen (Rice and Smoked Fish) ... 73
    Fufu (Congolese style) ... 75
    Pondu (Cassava Leaves) ... 77

Concetta Surtees – Life of Gratitude ... 78
    Chilli Cream Pasta – A delicious family recipe ... 82

Catriona Devlin – Serving as a Brigidine Sister ... 83
    Vegetable risotto (Vegetarian) ... 91

Gai Scrivens – A Walk with Nelson Mandela ... 92
    Vegetable Patties with Chutney ... 100
    Dhania Jeeru Indian spice ... 101

Sweets

Audry Hurley - Doves of Peace ... 102
    Elsie's Plum Bread ... 107

Beth Treacy – A Jewish girl ... 108
    Lemon Yoghurt Cake ... 113

Josephine Wane - Gratitude ... 114
    Cassava Pudding - A favourite of the Solomon Islands ... 118

Titilope Alao - Spirituality ... 119
    Puff Puff (Deep fried Dough) ... 128

Ingrid Hindell - From Catholic to eclectic

In 1950, I was born in Sri Lanka in the rural town of Kurunegala, nestled in the foothills of the Central Highlands which is 75 km from the capital city, Colombo. When I was five years old, my mother took me to England for seven months. I entered a hospital school where I undertook intensive physiotherapy so that I could hold my head up. My parents, my two grandmothers, my older brother and I immigrated to Australia when I was ten years old. I already had two aunts who had immigrated to Melbourne. My parents wanted to give their children a good education, but especially myself, because I was born disabled with cerebral palsy (CP). My parents were told by the Australian government that I would not get a pension until I was 20 years old, whereas my friends at the Marathon Spastic School in Malvern received a pension at 16 years of age. My parents were extraordinary in that they insisted that I get a good education. To help our family manage, we were supported by friends and relatives, especially my grandmothers. My parents were definitely enlightened people.

I always tell people that I'm disabled by CP. Building environments often do not allow access to my wheelchair. I'm a member of my community because I'm always in and out of meetings involving my community. But I'm not a member of my neighbourhood because many houses are inaccessible to me. This is called the 'social model of disability.'

I would like to offer a message about becoming empowered. The best way to explain it, is through a story about a friend who offered to help clean my house. I went to the bathroom and saw her using Ajax cleaner on the bathtub. I explained to my friend, "Yes, the bath could be cleaner, but my husband and I prefer not to use harsh chemicals." If a person tries to keep their ground, then repeat your response again, without raising your voice or showing anger or frustration, until your friend complies with your wishes. The empowerment steps are:

Herstory

1. *Begin your sentence by acknowledging what the other person just said with, "Yes, ..."*
2. *Use 'I could' instead of 'I must' or 'I should.'*
3. *Use 'I prefer' instead of 'I want.'*
4. *Never raise your voice in frustration.*

When I was 16, my very Catholic grandmother who was a lovely, gentle lady passed away. She taught me my catechism before I could hold my own head up, which as I mentioned occurred when I was five years old. She lived with us and helped with cooking in our home. By the 1960s, I had 17 cousins living in Victoria and most of my cousins had left the church. At 18 years of age, I did year 11 and studied Renaissance and Reformation European history. Through my studies, I discovered the history and politics of the church. I learnt that: priests were not allowed to get married after the 10th century and it seemed to be a purely economic position, because the 3rd and 4th sons of noble men were going into the church and enabled the church to become rich and powerful; French Huguenots and the Lombard's were massacred, and the pope only became 'infallible' in the 1870s when he was forced to give up his princely status of the Papal States when Italy became unified. Such things put me off the church. My parents were Catholics, but were also scientifically-minded and this had an influence as well. I did not see how to reconcile science and religion within myself. Like a typical teenager, my studies tended to weaken my link to the church, and I stopped going to church all together.

For some years afterwards in my 20s, I went to the Spiritualist Church near my home and it was then that I became interested in Eastern religion and Eastern philosophy. The Spiritualist Church was very influenced by the philosophy of Annie Besant who was a theosophical leader. To my delight, I found that the Spiritualist Church was 'marrying' Eastern and Western philosophies together, and that really resonated with me. I read books by Alan Watts, Bishop Shelby Spong and Llyal Watson who as a biologist and spiritualist, wrote Supernature. In my early 30s, I started going to the Unity Church and I found to my delight, that the Unity founders (the Fillmores) had direct links to Louisa M. Alcott who wrote Little women and many of my other favorite children's books. The Melbourne Unity Church had a very charismatic leader, and he and his wife were very good teachers of Unity metaphysics. To make the Bible come to life and relevant to people's lives today, Unity teaches the Bible by illuminating the meaning of Hebrew words. For instance, the name 'Isaac' means 'He (God) laughs.' The Jewish words give rise to different thoughts, and different thoughts give rise to different emotions.

In L. M. Alcott's books, the lead women characters were my friends when I was a teenager and young adult. I did not have many friends outside my family because I was very shy. I also did not go to university because it was too great a jump from my small 'special school.' It was too great a shock to my system. I refused to go to a sheltered workshop. In my 30s I decided to go to university off campus. I did three to four years of religious studies. My Bachelor of Arts major in International Relations took nine years to accomplish because I read widely about spirituality and metaphysics. I didn't do a second major in Religious Studies because my professor would not let me do a final essay on the Unity Church and its links to all the major world religions. One book in my university course was called *The world's religions*, by Houston Smith. He is such a brilliant writer that I used this one book as one of the references for all my Religious Studies essays, and after reading each chapter on a specific religion, I wanted to follow that particular 'wisdom tradition.' The Unity philosophy is linked with Hinduism, Buddhist concepts, Christianity and Judaism. Having Asian roots, the Unity philosophy sits well with me.

I met Robert Hindell (my husband) through an advertisement I placed in the newspaper, The Australian Singles News, in August of 1983. I was as honest as possible and I received 16 replies. I told each of these 16 men that I was disabled, and five people said that they still wanted to meet me. Robert and I both felt comfortable with each other. This comfortableness that we have for each other is unsurpassed. We lived together for six years and married in March of 1992.

In 1997, in my 40s, Robert and I moved to Geelong and I joined the Geelong Interfaith Group. I now call myself an eclectic, mainly because of what I learnt at the Unity Church and reading many books, particularly, The pagan Christ, by Tom Harpur; The Jesus sutras. Rediscovering the lost religion of Taoist Christianity, by Martin Palmer; The taboo against knowing who you really are, by Alan Watts, and The world's religions, by Houston Smith. If I have any words of wisdom to pass on, please read these books with an open mind and open heart.

Far-east Hommus

INGREDIENTS

1 tsp chili poweder
1 cup olive oil
4 tsp sweet paprika
2 tsp cardamom
2 tsp coriander
2 tsp cumin
2 tsp salt
1 tsp pepper
1 or 2 cloves garlic
2 cups dried chickpeas
1 cup Jalna plain yoghurt
1 cup tahini
Juice of 2 medium-large lemons

Slow cooker chickpeas

Blending chickpeas

METHOD

1. Soak chickpeas and then cook chickpeas until tender. It makes 5 cups of cooked chickpeas. Blend until they are smooth. Add all other ingredients.

2. NB – Lemon juice, yogurt and oil can be used to assist the blending process of the chickpeas.

Miti Tangianau - A Travelling Journey

I was born in the Cook Islands of the South Pacific, but my mother moved to Queensland, Australia when I was older. Once, when I was visiting her, I met someone who introduced me to the philosophy of the Family Federation for World Peace and Unification (FFWPU) and I studied the Divine Principle. I thought, "Oh, that's how it should be." I was going to go on my merry way back to the Cook Islands, but I got the chance to travel up and down Australia with the organisation. God offered me the opportunities to go travelling; that was very interesting and I loved it.

I have been really lucky. I love travelling and this is what I have been able to do. From 1989, I was living in South Korea and working as a missionary. The first missionary visa lasted three months, so I went to Japan and the visa was extended for a year. Then, every year, I went down to Pusan and caught the ferry across to Shimonoseki, Japan. Once I went to Japan in spring and visited Tokyo. Seeing the cherry blossoms in the park was just an amazing sight. I feel that God has supported my desire to travel and to learn about different cultures.

In 1992 when Dr. Hak Ja Han Moon opened the Women's Federation for World Peace (WFWP) International in South Korea at the Olympic Stadium, I was still living in Seoul, so I was able to attend and caught up with some Australians who came over just for the inauguration. I saw the beginning of WFWP International in the stadium and it was really fantastic. After the inauguration, Dr. Moon gave speeches in the major cities of South Korea and then began an international tour, giving keynote addresses in many countries. I was able to see some of the speeches when I was in Korea. I managed to find some money and paid the fare to go through France and then catch the train over to Great Britain. I went straight to Ireland and invited people to come to Mother Moon's speech. It was really exciting. We lived in a farm for a month and then I travelled back to France.

Herstory

My girlfriends said, "Miti. Do you want to come to America?" "Okay, I'm going to America," I thought. I had an open ticket and because of this, I was grilled at the airport about how long I going to stay in America, what my plans were, did I have any money on me, and how was I going to live in America. Anyway, after many hours, I received a one-month pass to stay in America, and I lived in Chicago with a couple who were missionaries to Egypt. After the month was up, I returned to France because my open ticket was a return ticket to France. I landed at the Charles de Gaulle Airport in France and as I was walking out from immigration, Dr. Hak Ja Han's party was also coming through. I was able to see her speech that same evening in Paris.

I joined in with the WFWP preparation team who were going ahead and supporting Dr. Moon's international speaking tour. The next morning after Mother Moon's talk in Paris, a bus was heading for Geneva to prepare in Switzerland. So I got on the bus, and off I went to Switzerland and listened to True Mother giving her speech there. From there, we went back to France and after a couple of days, I flew off to Egypt with the missionary couple I stayed with in Chicago. Meanwhile, Dr. Moon was continuing her European tour, going to countries such as Latvia and the Eastern European countries.

In the 1990s, Egypt was very restless and there were guards with guns at the airport; it was the first time I saw this type of situation. We were arranging the logistics for Dr. Moon's speech and sending invitations out by mail. However, a week before the speech date, we received word that maybe Dr. Moon wouldn't be able to come to Egypt because of the political tension, as it was very intense. I had a sudden realisation that I'm in Egypt, a place with a lot of Biblical stories. At that time, Mrs Sugiyama was the International WFWP President. She arrived in Egypt and we waited for a visa to be granted to Dr. Moon. Finally, one of the World Peace Academy professors assisted in getting Dr. Moon a visa, and she received a government escort from the airport to the hotel where she was going to speak. The government also provided security guard protection for her. The conference centre where Dr. Moon gave her speech was packed out with over a thousand guests.

Due to my ticket situation, I came back to Korea because I was living in Korea at that time. I decided to come back to Australia because my open ticket was almost at its end and Dr. Moon was coming to Sydney on the Oceania leg of her world tour. I thought, "I'll follow her back to Sydney." It was the end of 1993. My journey was really amazing. At one point I felt, "Oh, my gosh. Here I'm travelling around the world and following Mother Moon's speaking tour at the same time."

In 2007, the WFWP conducted an international conference at a mountain resort in North Korea. This was really an incredible feat. Four WFWP members from Melbourne went. People told us, "Oh it's dangerous to go, being a communist country." When we arrived at the airport in North Korea, there was an eerie kind of silence; we really stood out and could not talk to anyone. The guards didn't speak to us, and the North Korean people were not allowed to interact with us. During the WFWP conference, there was a Bridge of Peace Ceremony between the North and South Koreans, and afterwards everyone held lighted candles. The whole atmosphere was truly beautiful. Holding his or her candles, everyone sang the Tong-il unity song. We even went mountain climbing in Diamond Mountain, one of the beautiful mountain ranges in North Korea.

I always felt God really helping me. I love travelling, so at any opportunity, I'm jumping in, I'm there. In May 2004, I also went to Jerusalem, for the Middle East Women of Peace Conference, which was sponsored by the Inter-religious and International Federation for World Peace and WFWP International. The conference brought together 526 women from 41 nations. We visited Israeli and Palestinian victims of violence at Hadassah Hospital, plus the Yad be Yad Bilingual School, giving gifts and a financial donation. There was a Bridge of Peace Ceremony resulting in approximately 200 pairs of 'Sisters of peace.' Everyone returned home deeply touched, renewed and changed. Women are not usually allowed in a mosque, but we were able to. We visited the Dome of the Rock – yes, where Abraham took Isaac and put him on the altar. We did a march for peace through the Old City of Jerusalem. We even went to the Mount of Olives in the Garden of Gethsemane, and on a boat in the Sea of Galilee. This trip expanded my mind, seeing all the different cultures of East and West, Muslim, Jewish and Christian people all brought together at the conference. It was a fantastic multicultural hub.

I have enjoyed my travels and there's still more to come. It's always been 'my thing' to travel the world and experience life in different countries. I feel a lot of growth through the experience of travelling, living in different countries and learning about each other's cultures. That's part of my spiritual journey; visiting and sharing with people, I just love it. Through the Women's Federation and connecting to Mother Moon's later speaking tours, I also went to Las Vegas on one occasion.

My favourite recipe is a Korean seaweed soup called Miyeok; it is very nourishing. Korean people tend to like it really bland, just with seaweed. I like mine with beef, so I usually add beef, onions, garlic and ginger. Thank you. My spiritual journey is also my journey of travels.

Seaweed Soup A La Miti

INGREDIENTS

500g of diced chuck steak
150g of dried seaweed
2 large cloves of garlic
1 tbsp of crushed ginger
2 large onions
1 ½ - 2 litres of filtered water
Vegetable spice to taste

Serves 4

METHOD

1. In a deep frying pan, heat the oil.
2. Add beef and brown meat.
3. Chop onions and garlic and add to the frying pan.
4. Cook until onions soften then add crushed ginger.
5. Add seaweed and then a little water.
6. Transfer everything into a deep sauce pan.
7. Add the rest of the water slowly.
8. Cook until it boils and then simmer for an hour or until the meat is tender.
9. Add vegetable spice to taste.
10. Best served hot by itself or as a starter to a Korean Bulgogi meal with all the traditional side dishes.

Jacinta Darbishire - A rebellious spirit

Good afternoon everybody. My maiden name is Jacinta Miller; now I'm Jacinta Darbishire. I was born in Melbourne but was brought up in Alice Springs in the bush. I had a pretty privileged background, in that my parents did very well financially during the 60s and 70s when my Dad invested in a cattle station. He was also a pilot and delivered mail and medical supplies to the outlying stations in the entire Northern Territory and parts of Queensland and Western Australia. I grew up with my Dad going back and forth; sometimes he was at home and sometimes he was not. My Mum was born in England and flew out to Australia in 1948 from England in a two-seater biplane to be with my Dad. Imagine an English lady holding the fort alone and adjusting to life in outback Australia. My mother was the daughter of a British submarine commander, Rawdon Fletcher, and her mother was a spiritualist and poet named Margaret Smith-Sligo. My maternal grandmother was born in Scotland and lived in Malta and New Zealand in her youth. Both my grandmother and my mother were proud Catholics, and my grandfather was a convert.

My mother was ill a lot of the time after the birth of each of her four children because she was a coeliac and didn't find out the source of her illness until she was in her 60s. However, she loved dancing, Scottish country-style and ballroom. She also loved camping in the bush and looking after baby animals. Both my parents were fun-loving and adventurous, as well as having a strong religious streak. They allowed us a lot of freedom in our childhood; we lived outside a lot, swimming and pretending to be bushrangers. During the school holidays, I used to play in the bush with my brothers and sister, and each September, I had the opportunity to go on stock camp with stock hands who 'drove the cattle,' branded them, castrated them and got them ready for sale. I had a very wonderful opportunity to sleep in a swag, ride horses all day and eat out of a stockpot that continued as our meal stew base all week. As a kid, I took those

Herstory

things for granted. When I turned ten, my parents sent me to boarding school because they were quite strong Catholics and wanted me to get a religious education. I went to Loreto Convent in Adelaide. Even though it was a bit of a shock initially, I had an amazing time. It was an all-girls school, and because I was a fairly independent person, I really enjoyed it. Unfortunately, the one drawback was that I did not feel quite as close to my family as I would have liked.

However, I think all things happen for a reason, and I'm not resentful about boarding school; it gave me a lot of resilience I was brought up with the Catholic faith, which in the 50s was pretty separate from other Christian denominations. There was a deep distrust between Catholics and Protestants, but during my high school years, everything began to change.

During the early 60s, the Vatican II occurred when Pope John Paul announced the creation of the second Vatican Council. My Dad was very conservative and would call anybody who had new ideas a heretic. We were good friends with the local priest, and he used to come over and drink whisky with my Dad. My Dad used to throw him into the pool, and we all had a grand old time. Anyway, my parents were very much a part of the Catholic community in Alice Springs, and having a strong faith, we sometimes did prayer conditions called novenas where we would pray for nine consecutive days. It is like a chant where you say the Rosary over and over again. I remember it well because people would come to the door just before dinner every night and I hated it. We said a prayer together as a family when people would come around for drinks; they'd knock at the door, and Mum and Dad would say, "Don't come in, we're doing our prayer." I used to think, "This is so embarrassing. How can they do that?" Remembering it now, I think that my parents had such a stubborn, religious streak.

After Sunday Mass, my mother would stay back in church and pray while the rest of us were talking and catching up with our friends. My Mum never did that; she stayed in the church and prayed, and I used to think it was so embarrassing; it was so spiritual and religious. However, later on, I realised these experiences were resources, similar to money in the bank. I couldn't be like my Mum; I've never been able to pray very much in a long and consistent way. That was the way my mother was, and I'm very grateful for that somehow; she did something to help me by being like that.

I went to a Catholic boarding school with nuns around me. They really inspired me because they read the lives of the saints to us after dinner every night and it was really interesting. In primary school, we learnt about the ancient saints who got martyred back in the first thousand years of Christianity. But in high school, the Loreto nuns read modern saint stories; for example, Father Damien Molokai, working in the Pacific Islands and helping the lepers; amazing people in Vietnam, Laos, and communist Russia who died trying to stand up for the faith of Christianity under persecution from communists. My Dad was very strongly anti-communist.

On my Dad's side, my great, great grandfather, William Henry Miller, was the first white man to establish a convict settlement in Redcliffe in 1823, now known as Brisbane. He took 36 convicts with him and they tried to set up a farm; but nothing grew, and after a year, he was replaced by Captain Logan who was a cruel tyrant. My great, great grandfather retired from the British 40th Foot Army and settled in Tasmania. He had four children and was the son of a Presbyterian minister in Belfast. His photo shows him to be a pretty tough guy, and he fought with Wellington in a lot of his campaigns; but Australia was the last straw. I think he missed the camaraderie of the British Army. His eldest son worked with the Henty Brothers in Western Victoria, working bullock drays and profiting from the Ballarat gold rush by supplying goods. He became very wealthy and settled in Melbourne.

My Dad was a very adventurous person and loved the great outdoors; I got my adventurous spirit from him. My father was brought up in Melbourne as the only child of a second marriage between my 56-year old grandfather and my 16-year old grandmother. One was Protestant and one was Catholic; everything about that relationship was shunned by Melbourne society. My Dad suffered greatly due to this persecution and didn't have a lot of friends. He also had a physical deformity; he was born with a harelip and his parents refused to give him an operation until he was ten. He looked like an animal for the first ten years of his life; he had a face like a dog. I try to imagine that sometimes. I just can't imagine how awful that would have been. My grandfather's family was quite wealthy, making money from real estate during the gold rush. They were one of the richest families in Melbourne. My grandfather was very good with money, so even though he was disowned for marrying a young Catholic woman at the age of 56, he was already a wealthy young man. He'd already been through one marriage with a very successful Protestant lady who died of diabetes. His family must have thought he was mad; I can't imagine it. As an intelligent, young man, my father was quite wild; he used to drive a 40-98 Vauxhall too fast, and once in the 1930s, he ran into a herd of cows on Bourke Road in Melbourne.

I think back on what my parents did and the harsh circumstances they went through, and I realise it has created in me the feeling of being a rebel. My

Dad was pretty harsh; he was very authoritarian. During the war, my Dad was a pilot and flying instructor. He learnt to fly and he taught people to fly. He believed in military training and he brought us up like that; but we always fought against him. It was almost like we were testing our strength against him; we were like developing spiritual muscles by fighting with Dad. It was very hard to fight with my Dad because he was so strong and a really scary person. I never got to really know him well until a few years before he died, and I understood him more after he passed away. But that's another story.

When I was 20 years old, I had a vivid dream. I dreamt communism was a great idea and I was so pleased to be into communism because Dad was so against it. Nothing like stirring up your parents; so I thought, "Sounds like a good plan." Therefore, I joined the communist party, marched against the Vietnam War, and went to their meetings. I saw the way they behaved and thought, "They're disgusting people." I hated the way the communists were so violent in their talk and were very arrogant people. So even though I was sympathetic with the communist cause, I turned back to Jesus. I had a personal relationship with Jesus that I'd developed myself. Well, the Catholic faith tried to impose it on me, but it didn't work exactly the way they had planned because Jesus came to me independently through nature, art and books. That's really how I developed my relationship with God, and I was very grateful for this. I was quite independent and nature-loving, and believed that Jesus would return as a revolutionary, spiritual communist or something similar.

Helen, my older sister, was a wonderful source of inspiration for me. She taught me how to read and how to sing. I was singing in five different choirs and doing a cappella from the age of 13. We would sing five-part harmony rounds while doing the washing up. She was such a source of inspiration to me and I'm truly blessed by her presence. There are a lot of good mentors in my life and my sister was one of them. My Mum couldn't really talk or relate to me, even though she was spiritual person, and she didn't read much herself, not being a book person. My sister was brilliant and continues to learn languages. I think she's on her eighth language at the moment.

I was born a twin; my dear twin brother, Paul, followed me 30 minutes after I was born. We are not the same at all; different eggs, different spirit and everything. Paul is very gentle, kind, non-rebellious, sweet-natured and a dreamy person. He's adventurous in that he went on a bike trip through East Timor, learnt the Indonesian language, and has a heart for the faithful people he meets and lives with. He has an amazing memory, and he thinks and cares a lot about other people. He was my Mum's favourite. He has a great wit and is naturally funny. I now reflect on how I was pretty unkind to him during my youth, and I probably spent a bit of time bullying people like Paul. One year during high school, we had a new nervous teacher. I could feel myself wanting to make her leave and make life as difficult as possible for her so that she would leave. I had an animal instinct – that if you're not good enough, you've just got to drop out of the nest and make way for someone who is good enough. Seriously, that was what I was like; I had so much instinctive, survival mentality. I remember when the teacher did leave with a nervous breakdown, I felt so bad about it. There were other students who also joined forces with me, and I realised the power of unity against somebody. Really awful. When I left school, I didn't want to go to university straight away and went back to Alice Springs to work. I was involved in a play and played the role of Mary Magdalene.

During the 70s, I went to a university in Melbourne. I was going through a period of spiritual intensity and search. I had so much going on inside of me. My sister gave me books about the meaning of life such as Jack Kerouac's poetry and prose, Allen Ginsberg and the poets and what was happening in the west coast of America. I was thinking, "Wow, this is so interesting and it's really relevant to what's happening in Australia – why we're unhappy and in a state of revolution." I was trying to figure things out. At that time, I read Memories, dreams and reflections, a book about the life of a famous dream analyst, Carl Gustav Jung. He was a psychologist who interpreted dreams and realised that there were archetypes in every religion and culture, and a unifying set of archetypes or symbols. He wrote an amazing book called Man and his symbols. I was so excited that I thought I was going to burst out of my skin. I felt I was on the brink of a huge new world that was about to happen. I was so excited about it, that I took two years leave from university and travelled around Europe with my brother, Paul. To not get hassled, we pretended to be husband and wife, and we had a ball. We met a lot of people and did a lot of thinking.

I have an interesting story about a visit to the Vatican. Going into the main church, I saw a confession light on. I had been fighting with my parents at the time, so I thought I would confess my sin of hatred towards my parents. I went into the confessional and said, "I really hate my parents. What are you going to do about it? Can you help me?" The priest replied in English, "Oh my child, you must say three Hail Marys and three Our Fathers, and things will get better." I thought, "This solution is not relevant to my situation." I got out of the confessional and I felt an amazing sense of liberation, because the priest's response answered the prayer that I had been asking for years and years about my faith. To be honest, I was telling everybody that I was an atheist because I wanted to see what people would say to defend their faith. I wasn't really an atheist. But I pretended to be, playing the devil's advocate to find out people's reasons for their belief. Was it better than my reason? After my experience at the confessional, I walked with a sense of liberation across the Vatican square and I felt, "I'm going towards my future." Outside the Vatican, a bookshop displayed Memories, dreams and reflections, by Carl Gustav Jung. I bought the book, read it and I felt, "Wow, I'm being guided. I know I'm being guided." I knew I was being guided ten years ago, but today, I have even more proof; it is an amazing feeling.

Six months after I returned home from the European tour, I met a German girl. I was studying occupational therapy at university. At university we were studying rats and Skinner boxes as a way of understanding people's behaviour. I thought, "This is not enough; it's just not true. We're not just rats." I was so annoyed that I put my hand up and said to the lecturer, "I really don't like the fact that you're teaching us about rats in relation to human consciousness, and I'm not coming back to your program until the next interesting point. So if you don't mind, I'm leaving." I got up from the lecture theatre and everybody cheered. I don't know why they were into cheering; it was the 70s after all. I thought, "Right I'm going downtown." I don't know why I wanted to go downtown because I didn't believe in shopping. I was a hippy; I wore my sarong, rode a bike, I wasn't even eating chocolate and had abandoned all the things related to living a decadent lifestyle. (Everybody chuckled.) I was searching for the truth; I walked through the streets hating all the shops and hating all the materialism and feeling, "Where are you God?" A very conservative, German girl came up to me wearing a plaid coat because it was winter, and she said, "What would you like to see changed in the world?" I thought, "Maybe I'll just admit that I'm Christian." But I said, "We should all became real Christians and nice to each other all of the time." She replied, "Can you ever imagine that the purpose of Jesus returning was to create the true parents and true family of mankind that was lost due to the fall?". Bam! This hit me like a truck.

Wow, that was so relevant and I thought, "Wow, she is saying something so true." She looked so conservative, but invited me to study the Divine Principle and I said, "I've never done that before." I thought, "I've never done that before, it's a bit weird." I guess I'm a bit conservative about my own way of doing things so I said, "No, I don't think so." But all the voices in my head were saying, "Go. Find out what she is talking about; you're too fearful, you're just fearful and wimpy like all the people you hate." I was accusing myself of being fearful and wimpy while we went on chatting. Then she asked me again to study the Divine Principle and I said, "Okay." I went back to her house. It was a beautiful, little house and we had tea. She briefly taught me chapter one, two and three of the Divine Principle, and I thought, "Wow. This is making so much sense." She asked me to commit to returning to study further and gave me Young Oon Kim's book.

I was staying in a flat with my twin brother who, at the time, was trying to become a monk. I really wanted to study with this lady, even though she was a bit conservative looking. I loved all of the ideas even though I wasn't a very religious person; my brother was the religious one. I felt I wasn't very obedient; I just did what I liked and was fairly selfish. I felt that I had to find out about the Divine Principle and the founder. He's the one; the revolutionary who's going to change the world, the one we've been waiting for. I decided to study further and told my brother. He didn't even react; it was like he was in a dream and wasn't even listening. That was the beginning of my life in the Unified Family, which later became the Family Federation for World Peace and Unification (FFWPU). It was 1974. It must have been about six months later when I finished doing the intensive study of the Divine Principle.

I bore the karma of treating my parents in a cavalier manner during my teenage years later on, because in 1980, my parents tried to deprogram me. They thought I was in some terrible cult and had been influenced by various people who should have known better. I got into a really huge fight with my parents, and internally, I realised I was really torn that we couldn't achieve any resolution. It made me deal with my anger, resentment and forgiveness. I hated my parents so much and so intensely for trying to deprogram me that I had to purge it out of my body. I did this by writing letters of forgiveness over and over and over again. It was really hard, but it helped.

When I look back on my life, I know that everything that has happened to me has happened for a reason. Today I'm a domestic cleaner and work for people of an Indian, Sri Lankan and Chinese background. I'm really grateful to serve them because I know that my ancestors treated them badly. I'm grateful for the opportunity to feel any kind of resentment they might have towards me as a white Anglo-Saxon. Racism and trust barriers that divide the world due to religion and concepts attached to skin colour have created reasons to hate people. My life in the Family Federation is a way to work within myself and eliminate barriers, and to create a foundation for a better world. I believe that everything I do helps to create a better culture for people in the future. My ancestors did a lot for me; they made me tough and adventurous and have a respect for God. Through the Divine Principle, I've learnt the heart of God and feel a resolution to deal with the results of the fall which needs to be turned around so that we all can move forward with emotional and spiritual health.

I got married to a wonderful English man. He helped me deal with men, which was one of my bugbears. I think this came from a few women in my past who had a lot of issues with men. I'm very grateful to be married to a person like Ian because even his flaws are lovely. I'm willing to persevere because I got married for spiritual reasons. We were matched by Rev. Dr. Sun Myung Moon and when my husband and I met each other, we fell in love. The motto for our marriage and blessing was 'world peace through ideal families.' For myself, the family is not just an individual, nuclear family, it's the world family. We don't want to have borders anymore; we don't want to feel we're privileged or entitled to some lifestyle that other people are not entitled to. I have two children. It was a miracle that I gave birth and I'm very grateful for my mother-in-law's help with my physical health problems. She got me sorted out health-wise, and I managed to have two children before I became too old. I was 36 when my son was born, and 42 when my daughter was born. Both of them are showing all the rebellious streaks that I've had, but I think they're a lot more thoughtful and intelligent. I can't criticise them at all, because I was the same. I just want to be there for them and achieve my goals so that my success will carry forward to help them.

Jacinta's Recipe on next page.

Spring Kimchi Salad

INGREDIENTS

3 cups Chinese cabbage (finely shredded) **or baby Bok Choi** (cut into individual leaves)
3 tbsp sea salt
3 spring onions (finely shredded)
1 clove of garlic
½ tsp Korean red chilli powder
1 tbsp sesame oil
1 ½ cups water

Serves 4

METHOD

1. Finely shred the Chinese cabbage or separate the baby Bok Choi into individual leaves.
2. Mix the water and salt until the salt is dissolved.
3. Soak the finely shredded cabbage or Bok Choi in the salty water and leave for 15 minutes.
4. Rinse the cabbage or Bok Choi twice and shake out the water.
5. Mix this with the remaining ingredients (spring onions, garlic, sesame oil and chilli).
6. For a richer flavour, allow to stand for 24 hours. But it does work served immediately.

Lucy Verstegen - Beautiful music

Hi all, my name is Lucy Verstegen. I celebrated my 85th birthday a few weeks ago here in beautiful Australia. I was born in Holland in 1930 and am trying to remember back to the time when I was little. I was born to elderly parents who were in their 40s when I came along. My father was a widower when he married my Mum. He had a son who was 15 years old when I was born, and this young man was like a second Dad to me. For the purpose of this talk, I will focus on the religious aspect of our family. My father was Protestant, although I don't remember him ever going to church when I was little. My mother, who lived in Paris during her early adulthood, was French Protestant and attended a French girl's school in her teen-years. She spoke fluent French and tried to teach me to do the same. However, I forgot most of it in Australia because no-one here speaks French. When I was 17, my mother passed into Higher Life. She did not enjoy good health, and for her, it was a blessing when she was taken into the next life.

My father formed new friendships; he was interested in politics and tried to fix the world's problems in that way. When I was about 20, a friend invited my father to come along to a Lutheran Church; he was Lutheran and very happy in that religion. So my father went with him, was very impressed and then talked me into going with them. In that way, I was introduced to the Lutheran Church in Holland, which is based upon the church in Sweden. It is totally different from the experience we had in the Lutheran Church in Australia later on. I was baptised and confirmed as a Lutheran. The minister was fantastic, and years later, I realised he was a medium and worked with spirit guides, but at the time, I didn't know and perhaps no-one in his congregation did. In the meantime, my brother got married and had two beautiful, little kids and decided to move and live in Australia.

It was a great family upheaval. After two years, my father decided he wanted to be with his son, so the two of us came to Australia also. This was in 1958, and it was a life-changing experience for us, as it is for anyone who packs up and moves to another country. My brother lived in Springvale and we moved there too. My father and I wanted to go to church somewhere. On the first Sunday in Melbourne, we visited a Presbyterian Church which later became the Uniting Church. The leader was an Irish minister; he was a very nice person, but I couldn't understand why I had to travel to the end of the world to be greeted by an Irishman. We stayed in the Presbyterian Church from 1958 until the late 70s. By that time, my father's health wasn't very good and he decided to stay home. I met a lady who invited me to come to her church, the Victorian Spiritualist Church (VSU) in the city. My mother had been interested in spiritualism, so it wasn't new to me. I went along with her and finished up staying there. At the time, however, I had become the part-time organist in the Presbyterian Church where a friend of mine was the full-time organist and singer. This church has a beautiful old pipe organ which is a joy to play. There aren't many pipe organs in Australia. Ian was a professional singer and I played for him during church events. He was very happy with that, because he studied singing and never had a pianist to play for him. I started to go to the VSU and sometimes there was a conflict of interest, because I needed to be in both places at the same time to play the organ. It's amazing how popular one can be if one plays an instrument. One weekend, somehow I managed to have a double appointment. I had to play in the Burke Road church for something, and I also had to be in the city. I said to the minister of the Uniting Church that I had a double appointment. I had to play for a wedding or something, and it was the first time that I mentioned the Spiritualist Church to him and he was NOT happy. He asked me where this church was and asked whether it was the one on A'Beckett Street. How did he know that anyway? He said to me, "Well, if you go there you won't have to come back here." Just like that. So I looked at him and said, "Okay." I thought if this is his interpretation of Christianity, what could I do? So I have never been back to the Burke Road church, which is very sad, because it is a lovely place and Ian was very upset, because of course, he didn't agree with me going to the Spiritualist Church.

Having been kicked out of the Burke Road church, I went to the Spiritualist Church from then on and stayed there until 1990. We had the same president for 23 years, or maybe even longer, I can't remember exactly. He was a wonderful medium, and his family was very lovely – father, mother and two kids. But he was a lot older than I was and he wanted to retire, which was fair enough. The trouble with Spiritualist Churches is that to be the president or the minister, one has to be a qualified clairvoyant and preferably a trance speaker as well. If you are not one of those, or preferably both, there is no way you will get the job. For two years this minister tried to find someone to take on his position, because it was a very big one. Eventually, when he was in his late 70s, he said, "Look, I have to get out of here, just do the best you can." Then the committee brought in a gentleman who knew very little about spiritualism. It was the end of an era, and things were not the same for some considerable time. Around that period, a group of people created an organisation called the Unification of Spiritualism and some of us who had left the VSU joined in. One lady in that group worked very hard. She had three churches to run in Boronia, Shepparton and Warburton. Eventually she asked me if I could take on the Warburton church, as it was becoming too much for her. That was how I became involved in the Warburton church. After two years of training, I was ordained as the minister and was accepted as such, by the Australian Government.

One year later I became a marriage celebrant, which was wonderful, because I could marry the people belonging to my Centre, and others as well. One sad case was a young couple who split up six months later. I was the minister for 12 years and had a wonderful time; we had a lovely community. We had a church in Warburton and eventually, another one in Alexandra near Mansfield. We looked for a vice-president to help me with this added responsibility and found a gentleman who was willing to help. Then one day, a couple who had been kicked out of three Spiritualist Churches in the city because of their drug use, came to live in Warburton. Lo and behold, they bought a house in Warburton and came with their drugs. In our Centre, we had a couple and a few young men in their 30s who thought it was cool to try out drugs with this new couple. One year later, the end result was I had to close the church. In a Spiritualist Church, if you are on drugs or anything that causes hallucinations, the wrong entities from the other side of life become attracted. Right from the beginning of Spiritualist Church studies, much emphasis is placed on the fact that church members have to be absolutely clean, with no use of alcohol or drugs. So I had to close the Centre, which was a great shame. All this happened around the same time as the 9/11 disaster, and the insurance for our Centre went up right through the roof. Before the 9/11 disaster, we paid $140 per year for insurance but then it went up to $1,140 per year. Well, there is no Spiritualist Church that can afford that, and within six months, four Spiritualist Churches closed; mine was one of them. But I think our basic problem would have been the drugs, as we could have conducted our service in someone's home. So that was that! By this time, I was 72 and exhausted, because it is jolly hard work running a Centre, especially as a single female. Like most of you will know who run churches, it is very hard work. At the same time, I was also teaching piano, because money had to come in. So I was doing the work of two professions. I was exhausted and needed to have a break. I waved goodbye to everybody and said, "I'm going to close the door on this. I will not see you later."

I lived in Belgrave, and just around the corner from where I lived is a beautiful property that had a little church on it. I think it was first a Pentecostal Church before it was taken over by a Rumanian Church. I walked a lot and often would go past this church. One day it was sold and became the Melbourne Family Church of the Family Federation for World Peace and Unification (FFWPU), the Unification Church. Although I walked past it quite frequently, I hadn't been in the church yet and was interested. However, on Sunday mornings I gave piano lessons to VCE students who couldn't come any other day. One day, I looked out of the window of my lounge room and there was half a meter of water in my front garden. As the level increased I phoned for help, but no-one came to the rescue. Then a lady from across the road came and enquired about what I was going to do about this, because by then, the street was full of water too. I told her that I had rung the SES, but so far the response had been unsuccessful. She offered to ring for me, and lo and behold, she did a better job than I did, because after ten minutes, the fire brigade arrived. Amongst the people who came was a very tall gentleman who reminded me of my father. My spirit guide said to me, "That's the one you go to." So I went up to this gentleman and I threw my arms around him and I cried, "Help." He turned out to be the minister of the church down the street. He gave me a little card and said, "Come over one day and meet my wife." I thanked him for everything.

The water issue was resolved; a pipe had burst in front of my house, and I put the minister's business card on my table. A couple of days later I picked it up and looked at it; it was from the Unification Church. As I mentioned, I gave piano lessons on Sundays and wasn't able to leave the house. But when Christmas came, the students had finished their exams by then and I was free. So on the New Year's morning of 2005, I got myself all dressed nicely; thank goodness my spirit guide told me to wear a long dress down to the floor. I walked up the long driveway of this little church that I had been seeing for some time, and arrived at the front porch. The porch was covered in shoes, and I stood there and looked at all those shoes. I had the distinct feeling that I had come 'home.' When I went inside, I noticed that everybody was dressed in oriental style and all in white; no-one was wearing their shoes. That was my first introduction to the FFWPU; the first day of January 2005, and I have been there ever since. It is very similar to spiritualism. There are some issues that are different and I used to get upset in the beginning, but I have put that away. And yes, I'm very happy. Beautiful people, we are all trying very hard to work for peace on earth, and foster good communication between different nations. Yes, I'm quite settled. I did omit a bit when I said I walked up the church path. Actually, I had met one of the ladies of the church. She was the wife of the previous minister and had come to my door to fundraise in August 2004. That lady and

I had become good friends, we still are and we always will be. It was through her that I first came to know the church and conducted a piano concert in the hall of the church with my students. That's how I came to know that there was a service on New Year's morning at seven o'clock. Otherwise, I wouldn't have known of course. It was a wonderful introduction to the Centre, and I have been there ever since. I'm very happy there, and hopefully will be there always.

I'm now in my 86th year. I don't attend Spiritualist Churches anymore, and I don't do any clairvoyance work. I have never been very good at that anyway. I used to go to a church in Preston (a Melbourne suburb) and do readings for people. The lady minister of that church used to get very upset with me, because when I gave people a reading, I most often talked about their animals. "I have your dog here," or "your cat," or "your horse," or whatever. This minister had a strong belief that people were only interested in their health and that I should only be talking about their health. But instead, I spoke about their dogs or cats or whatever I was guided to talk to them about. I love talking about the animals and therefore, that is what was usually given to me. I still remember a beautiful German Shepherd that belonged to a young man I gave a reading to. He was very happy when I spoke about his dog. Anyway, I don't do anything like that anymore. I'm now being spoilt by my sisters in the church. Thank you for your attention. Till next time, God bless you.

Lucy's Recipe on next page.

Gourmet open Sandwiches with Cheese

INGREDIENTS

2 slices of whole grain bread
Butter
1 egg
Ham, chicken or turkey
¼ onion (finely sliced)
Half a small avocado
Shredded/sliced cheese

Serves 1

METHOD

1. Preheat the oven to 180°C.
2. Line an oven tray with baking paper.
3. Butter both slices of the bread & place each slice butter side up on the oven tray.
4. Cook the egg, ham and onion in separate areas of the non-stick frypan so that they do not mix together.
5. Place the cooked onion on one of the bread slices. Sprinkle shredded/Sliced cheese over the onion to your liking.
6. Slice the avocado and place it on the second slice of bread.
7. Layer the egg and then the ham (chicken or turkey) over the avocado.
8. Sprinkle herbs, salt and pepper over one of the slices.
9. Place the tray in the oven for approx. 10-15 minutes until the cheese has melted.
10. Take the tray out of the oven and place the grilled slices part way open on a serving plate, as shown in the picture and serve warm.

Monica Zaman - Dreams in her eyes

My presentation is a little bit different; it is a story about refugees, asylum seekers and migrants when they come to their new country and what problems they face. Often they come alone. They face problems individually, plus their families also suffer. When I left my son in Pakistan four years ago in 2010, he was 17 years old; now he's 22. My family (my husband and son) just arrived in Australia last month. We are trying to understand each other and fill the gap due to the separation. It's very hard for families when they are away from each other.

Now, I will start my story. An ambitious girl in her early 20s went for her first interview after getting her master's degree. She was energetic, dreams were in her eyes, and she wanted to do something for humanity as a social worker, a value which she had learnt from her childhood Christian Church community and her studies in the Department of Social Work. She reached the interview room two hours before the interview was to start. She was sitting and praying, "Please God, help me. I need this job and through this job I want to help people."

When one of the panellists said, "You have no work experience, so how will you be able to work in this job?" I answered, "If I have no previous job experience and I need experience, how will I ever get a job? I have many plans for this job." The interviewers smiled and said, "Okay, we will let you know if you have been successful." After a few days, I got the job working with Afghan refugees. It was a very exciting job for me.

As a United Nations High Commissioner for Refugees District Coordinator, I was also given a car and a driver, and I started to work with the refugees in the camps. I cried every day because I had never seen such poverty and pain and so many people with problems.

Whenever it rained, I could not sleep at night, just thinking about the people who were living in the camps. Many times, I helped the people from my own pocket. A verse from the Holy Bible always comes to my mind for refugees: "God is our refuge and strength, a very present help when in trouble." I worked mainly with refugees living in camps. But after one year, I left the job because I got married and moved to another city.

I started my university career as a lecturer at Balochistan University, in Balochistan Pakistan. But I was ambitious and wanted to progress in my career, and therefore, started further study. I registered myself as a PhD student and during my studies, I won a merit scholarship to study in Germany. I finished my PhD on causative factors of mental retardation. The work titled Intellectual disability facts, is published in the USA and the UK in book form. Eventually, I became the head of department. I was always ambitious and did a lot of research, presented research papers at international conferences, and supervised master's and PhD research students. I was at the top of my desired career.

But no-one ever knows what can happen. I never thought that I would be working with refugees and then become a refugee myself. I understood that to become a refugee, or to seek asylum, was not a choice. Circumstances make a person a refugee or asylum seeker. Today I am here as a refugee because I have no other choice or identity.

When people introduce me, sometimes they introduce me as, "This is Monica, and she is refugee." Can I ask the audience here a question? Is this an introductory title for people? Whoever comes to a new country because of discrimination against their religion, caste, or colour, someone who has been persecuted and lived in fear of being killed, surely they have other identities? Then why this stigma? When I feel depressed or in stress, a verse always come into my mind: "He only is my rock and my salvation, my stronghold; I shall not be greatly shaken."

Since arriving in Australia four years ago, I have met many people who have refugee status and who face problems, most of whom other people never think about. Refugees face isolation because of language. They have no social life because they cannot travel due to lack of money and a limited knowledge of the country. They have psychosomatic disorders because of fear, stress and depression. They cannot sleep well because of nightmares. Sleeplessness and depression affects their appetite. Stress can lead to many physical diseases which, previously, they had never experienced.

Every day, newly arrived refugees wake up with new hope that maybe they will get a job today, their family will get their visas, and they will start a new life here in Australia. Refugees come alone; they miss their families, their children, husband, wife, parents and other siblings. They miss their culture, traditions, festivals and customary dress. But there was no other choice but for them to leave their homeland. The only way was to flee, escape, seek asylum and become a refugee. Every refugee and asylum seeker feels they are losing their identity in the new land; with a new society and new culture. Sometimes, they feel that they are misfits in this new culture and they have no identity.

When refugees or asylum seekers apply for a job and are unsuccessful, they feel that they are rejected and ignorant. To get a job in their professional field is like catching the moon. Many highly educated people start studying again and take certificate courses because this may be a qualification that the job market demands. But, after completing a course, they can still face problems in getting a job because of having no previous local experience. So they may start volunteer work. However, if they show their qualifications and previous experience at this volunteer workplace, people may not want to talk with them freely because they feel afraid that this person could take their job.

So after bitter experiences, many highly educated and professionally trained refugees retreat and build a shell around themselves. Do you know why? They are hurt and have lost their identity. They try to find a job so that they can pay their rent, bills and meet their basic requirements. When a person has lost their identity, it is the death of that person. They cry because they have not only lost their identity, they have lost their family, their country and everything. They feel like a lonely person, sitting in the middle of an island with no-one around.

A verse again from the Bible: "May the Lord reward your work, and your wages be full from the Lord, the God of Israel, under whose wings you have come to seek refuge."

Refugees do not suffer alone; their families back in their home countries suffer also. They miss each other in every area of life. I was not able to sleep, and my son sleeps with things that remind him of me, because then he feels that I am with him. I felt guilty about my loved ones. I missed my son and my husband. When I feel like this, I pray and read the Bible. Sometimes, I just pray and listen to religious songs because it gives me strength. I am a mother and a wife. I was a university professor and the head of department. But here, I am only Monica.

If I had felt safe in my homeland, I would never have experienced the stigma of being a refugee; but it is not a choice. Sometimes, I become frustrated and confused and ask myself, "Who I am? Who I am now? What is my identity?" Sometimes, people treat refugees like a dumb person. When this happens, I feel as though there is something broken inside me; my confidence or identity.

A verse from Bible: "But you, oh Lord, are a shield about me, my glory, and the one who lifts my head."

Asylum seekers and refugees are not permanently poor in health, wealth and knowledge; they are just disenfranchised for a short period due to lack of means and opportunities. Many are the cream of their countries; the new country should take advantage of their knowledge, skills and experience. Trust them and give them respect. They have left many things behind; help them to rebuild their lives. If they cannot speak English fluently, it doesn't mean that they are ignorant or intellectually inferior to other people. You do not need to speak louder to them, thinking that this will help them understand English better.

A verse from Bible: "God is our refuge and strength, a very present help in trouble."

Many organisations provide opportunities for refugees to learn many new skills, but with a few changes, they can also help to make them happier. Just provide them with the skills which are relevant to their previous profession or education, and believe me, they will try to find their place and rebuild their identity in that profession.

When I came to Australia, I was living in a women's hostel in Richmond. I started going to church and attended Bible study group. Sometimes I had no money to travel, but I walked from Richmond to Collins Street to attend Sunday service and Bible study group, whether it was raining, cold or in hot weather. My spiritual journey did not start in Australia; it started when I was born because my father was a minister. I was the oldest child in the family. As I grew physically, I grew in my spiritual life also.

While alone in Australia, I was lonely. In my refuge, God gave me strength and I always prayed, "Please give me my family." God heard my prayers, and my family received visas in May and came to Australia during the last week of May 2014.

I'm continuously growing in my spiritual life. I felt many changes in myself, my son and my husband. I'm trying to fill up the gap of being separated for three and half years. But I am happy for one thing – that our spiritual life has not changed. My son cannot read English perfectly so I was surprised when he said, "I can read the Bible because you taught me, and I can read all those verses and all those chapters. I learnt them by heart because you taught me when I was a child." It gave me happiness that he remembered the Bible verses.

When my son was a child, I always read and explained the Bible verses to him. Due to circumstances in Pakistan, you never know if you will come back home or not because of bomb blasts and suicide bombers. So, when I was here alone, I prayed on the phone or on Skype with them, and asked them to read Bible verses with me. We also thanked God that we were all growing in our spiritual life.

My spiritual journey has not stopped. I'm getting more strength from God every day because He heard my cries and praise. When I was alone and in depression, He gave me shelter and is providing for my livelihood through different sources, although I have no job.

A verse from the Bible: "For I was hungry and you gave me something to eat. I was thirsty and you gave me something to drink. I was a stranger and you invited me."

In my profession in Pakistan, I am a researcher. In Australia, I want to do research about asylum seekers and refugees and the problems their families face back in their home country. However, I have no funding. If, in the future, I get some funding or a scholarship, I want to work on this topic. I want to work for people who are facing problems and persecution in their home countries. I also want to highlight the problems refugees face in their new country. Such a study can help the Australian government understand problems such as very long delays in getting visas. What happens to the family back in the home country when they don't get their visa? Sometimes, this causes family breakup. Sometimes, half the family is in Australia and the other half is still in the home country. This causes psychological problems where the family does not accept each other; everything changes. So a study of the plight of families in such circumstances can be helpful for the Department of Immigration.

Questions and comments from the audience

Comment: I have a lot of thoughts. I think, in this country, the policy about refugees comes from the top-down. The way the government gets voted in, is to tell the population that refugees are bad, and by stopping the boats the government is a hero.

Comment: Governments don't really care either way about refugees. I think there are different levels of persecution. It's a lot easier for a white woman in a country like Australia; but there are levels of persecution for women in this country as well. Through my own experiences, I've suffered in my own way and prayed to God and found my way out. Therefore, I think I can really relate to what you're saying. Unfortunately for you, your experience is that many Australians have poor attitudes about refugees because there is a lot of ignorance; but there's a lot who don't think that way also.

Comment: I think the way for change in Australia is through education at the grassroots level, because the government is putting out a lot of propaganda against letting people into Australia. The best thing would be to give a lecture or talk from your own personal experience. There's a lot of work to be done, but I don't think you should give up because of that. I'm sorry that that's the way it is for refugees in Australia. It's the Western world; it's very cold.

Comment: When people are worried about money and their own jobs, they think that money is going to make them happy. People don't understand that we're all related, that we're all one family.

Monica: I have many bitter experiences and many good experiences. Once I was surprised when someone asked me, "Have you ever eaten a cake?" I'm a good cook, I bake many things. I started cooking classes here also. I was surprised that people have no knowledge about other countries; this is why I was asked such a question. The Pakistan sweets are amazing. This lady did not know about Pakistan. Many times I heard people say, "Don't trust refugees; they have nothing, they can steal from you, they can steal this, they can do that." When I was in Pakistan, I was teaching in the university. My husband is a civil engineer. My son studied in the best school in Pakistan. We were paying his fees in English pounds. I had a driver who drove me to university and brought me back. I never carried a work bag, a shopping bag or anything because my driver always carried everything for me. Here, I run after the tram.

Comment: Your children's children will have a different experience compared to you. You're the one who's breaking ground for the generations to come. From the refugee women I've met, when I hear somebody is a refugee, I'm just astounded by the amazing person I'm meeting. So when someone says, "This person is a refugee," it's a really positive thing to me. I think, "I see a survivor who's amazing and comes from the other side of the world." Eventually, we'll be able to turn that around. But for now, it's been hard for you and your family, so I'm sure it's not been great for you. Coming to Australia from a

European background, compared to Europe, I think Australia is the ideal melting pot. I think for the future, for the melting pot to take place, we need more information and education in the sense of explaining people's stories.

Comment: Even the government of today is not even able to retain and sustain this country by themselves; they're welcoming people with the highest education because the government needs them. But, how do you really differentiate between a terrorist or not? The government should not jail the refugees with their children.

Comment: I think Australians need to feel more empathy. As time goes on, I'm seeing a shift in the amount of empathy people have because there's more education about our refugee situation on the computer or Facebook, and people making friends with people from different backgrounds. My children have friends from all over the world.

Comment: Australia has received waves of refugees from specific countries. After a few years, the refugees become new Australians and settle. Then nobody thinks twice about it. They're Australian. It does get easier once people feel settled. We need to assist our refugees and lift them up because this is really their land also. By lifting them up, we lift ourselves up.

Comment: I'm Japanese. I didn't know until I came here, that Australia and Japan were enemy nations during the war. My second son was born here. He was asked, "Why are you here? Why have you come to this school?" He didn't say anything bad to people. He doesn't buy clothes much, and he saves his money. He went out looking for people who needed help and would give them money. In one newspaper article I read, "Don't give money to homeless people." But my son would say, "I have a roof, I have parents, so I'm very happy." Things change. When my friend came from South America many years ago, he received support from the government. However, our situation was so difficult; my husband was working so hard with two shifts per day to set up his business. Now he has become successful, so he donates money. We really try to be middle class, but we don't want to be above middle class. Every week we save money to give to other people.

Comment: The city where I work is very rich. Somebody was telling me the other day, that there's a high percentage of ten percenters living in this area. I asked, "What's a ten percenter?" I thought they meant ten percent of the richest people lived in the area. I found out that ten percenters are the people who own only ten percent of their belongings. There's a lot of the houses where you see people look as though they are wealthy and have a lot, but they don't. They only own ten percent. At my work we call it the house of cards that's ready to come down at any moment. They have empty fridges and they go to services looking for food. Their life is an illusion.

Monica: Thank you very much. Thank you very much for your support, for your kind words and sharing your own life experiences with me. I need your prayers for my family circumstances here; we all are looking for work. I started to educate myself again so my qualifications are recognised in Australia. I am gaining a Certificate IV accreditation in Management and Community Services, just to get a foot in the door so I can get a job. I need your prayers; please pray for my financial situation.

Monica's husband and son finally received their visas and immigrated to Australia in 2015; the united family lives in Melbourne.

Spiced Flatbread (Methi paratha)

MAKES: 8
PREPARATION: 30MIN
COOKING: 20MIN
SKILL LEVEL: MEDIUM

INGREDIENTS

Spice Mixture:
2 tsp vegetable oil
2cm piece ginger, finely grated
2 long green chillies, seeded, finely chopped
½ tsp cumin seeds
¼ tsp ground turmeric
¼ tsp salt
½ cup dried **Methi** (fenugreek leaves) (see note)
2 tbsp ghee
mint and tamarind chutney (podina), **to serve**

Paratha Dough:
1 cup wholemeal flour
1 cup plain flour
220ml warm water
2 tbsp ghee

METHOD

Spice Mixture:
1. Heat the oil in a frying pan over low heat and cook together the ginger, chillies and cumin seeds for 2 minutes or until the ginger is soft.
2. Add salt and turmeric, and stir until combined. Remove from the heat, stir in Methi and set aside.

Paratha Dough:
1. To make paratha dough, sift the flours together in a large bowl. Make a well in the centre and stir in the warmed ghee and the warm water until the mixture forms smooth dough; add more flour if necessary.
2. Knead in the spice mixture and then divide it into 8 balls. Roll each ball out on a lightly floured surface to make a 20 cm round.
3. Place the rounds on an oven tray lined with baking paper and cover loosely with plastic wrap to prevent drying out.
4. Heat a large heavy-based or non-stick frying pan over high heat. Working with one round at a time, cook dough for 2 minutes each side or until it starts to brown.
5. Drizzle with 1 tsp ghee and cook for a further 30 seconds or until golden, then flip and repeat on the other side. Repeat with remaining dough rounds.

Almond Stuffed Meatballs with Spicy Tomato Sauce

INGREDIENTS

Meatballs:

1 kg minced beef
1 egg, lightly beaten
1 onion, finely chopped
½ cup coriander leaves, chopped
5cm piece ginger, grated
1½ tbsp garam masala
½ tsp ground chilli
1 tsp salt
1 tbsp besan flour (besan flour is a chickpea flour that is less starchy than wheat flour. It is available from Indian food shops and selected supermarkets and greengrocers).
½ tsp saffron threads
30 blanched almonds, soaked in water for 2 hours
¼ cup oil, to shallow-fry
Coriander leaves and spiced flatbread (methi paratha), to serve

METHOD

Meatballs:

1. To make meatballs, soak saffron in 2 teaspoons of boiling water for 10 minutes, to soften.
2. Combine the ground beef, egg, onion, coriander leaves, ginger, garam masala, ground chilli and salt in a large bowl.
3. Using your hands, knead in besan flour until mixture is smooth and elastic. Knead in saffron and soaking liquid. Roll mixture into 30 balls.
4. Using your thumb, make a small indentation in the centre of each meatball. Place a drained almond into each indentation, then roll ball to enclose almond.
5. Place on a tray, cover with plastic wrap and refrigerate for 20 minutes.
6. Heat oil in a deep frying pan. Cook meatballs, in 3 batches, for 4 minutes, tossing occasionally, or until lightly browned. Drain on paper towel.

Almond Stuffed Meatballs with Spicy Tomato Sauce

INGREDIENTS

Curry Sauce:

3 tbsp ghee
2 onions, thinly sliced
4 garlic cloves, finely chopped
1 tsp ground turmeric
1 tsp ground cumin
700 g (about 5) tomatoes, chopped
½ cup natural yoghurt
½ cup water
1 tsp salt

METHOD

Curry Sauce:

1. Heat the ghee in a large heavy-based saucepan over medium heat. Add onions and garlic, and cook for 8 minutes or until golden.
2. Stir in turmeric, cumin, chopped tomatoes and yoghurt, and reduce heat to low. Cook for 10 minutes or until tomatoes soften.
3. Add meatballs, water and salt and bring to the boil. Reduce heat to low, cover, and cook for 10 minutes or until meatballs are heated and cooked through.

Transfer meatballs to a serving dish, scatter with coriander leaves and serve with curry sauce and spiced flat bread.

Naya (Barbara) Vondracek - A first generation Aussie

My birth name is Barbara Eileen Vondracek, which speaks of my ancestry. Barbara comes from my Austrian paternal grandmother, Barbara Dvorak, and from my mother's fondness of the actress, Barbara Stanwyck. The name Eileen nods to my mother's Irish heritage, and Vondracek originates from Prague and my father's Bohemian side of the family.

I'm a first generation Aussie who grew up in the Australian outback until I was 12 years old. My father, Karel, was one of ten children and born to Ludwig Vondracek, a fresco artist from Prague, and Barbara Dvorak from Vienna. Ludwig, my grandfather, received many artistic commissions from churches and public buildings. But during the night, he spent up big at the taverns, so my father's family didn't have a lavish life. Barbara, my grandmother, was a loving and devoted mother, and family was very important to them all. By the end of World War II, only two brothers and one sister remained alive, and obviously the war was hard on them. My father, Karel, was in the Czech cavalry and was captured, tortured and left for dead by the Nazis. He recovered, re-enlisted and was again captured; this time interned in a concentration camp. He escaped from the camp, and with others he met along the way, escaped to France across the mountains where he joined the French Resistance. He also got work as an undercover security guard in one of the big hotels on the Champs Elysees, which was owned by one of the families he'd helped to escape. Karel enjoyed a few years in Paris working and enjoying time at the Folies Bergeres and the Moulin Rouge.   Oooh-la-la.

Mama, by contrast, always said that after learning of Daddy's horrid wartime experiences, she felt guilty to say that she'd had the time of her life during the war. She was volunteering

Herstory

with Mrs Churchill's war effort in London, working hard and having a fun social time; forming life-long friendships, and eventually receiving a gold watch for her efforts that I have and still treasure. She'd had a rather bucolic and privileged upbringing in Carrick Fergus, Northern Ireland, where her father, Samuel Allely, an Orange man, had been a police officer, then an army officer during the Boer War and World War I. He also became a member of the Belfast City Council later in life. Her mother's mother, Maud Alice Talbot Plunkett Hussey de Berg, was a very God-centred Quaker who was very fond of, and always kind to the gypsies who travelled around Ireland with their colourful horse-drawn wagons full of trinkets, stories, music and laughter. She would feed them and give them clothes; they in turn would sell her trinkets and do fortune telling readings for her. She was told in one reading that her youngest daughter's, youngest daughter would see the end of the world as we know it; that would be me. There has always been the air of magic on my mother's side of the family. Mama had a son in Ireland before she came to Australia. I adore my brother, Desmond. He and his wife, Gloria, have three children who married into big country families in Victoria. Thus I have a real Aussie side to my family too, which I love and is such a contrast to the European side.

In this picture my father, Karel Vondracek, is on the far right.
It was taken during World War II when he joined the French Resistance.

The motto of my grandmother's family (Hussey) is, "Do unto others as you would be done by." From the Irish side, this motto, and a deep love for Jesus, was a cornerstone of my upbringing. I am also deeply grateful for the magic that flows to me from that dear land across the Irish Sea. From my father, also came advice that has guided me well. He said to me, "Darling, God is Love and God is in your heart, and any religion or philosophy or cult you come across that is not of Love, is not of God." Dad was not religious, but he was a spiritual man who found his peace and communion with God in nature. As a child, seeing the natural world through his eyes forged a touchstone for me to also find the peace that nature brings. My father had a green thumb, and our gardens were always magical places. He also had a way with animals and birds, and at one stage, he had a pet eagle. Animals were always, and still are a major passion of mine too. Mama took it hard when her parents passed. She wanted to get as far away from the memories as possible, so she bought a ticket for her and my brother, Desmond, to travel on a ship heading to the Antipodes. Papa wanted to get as far away as possible from the memories and threat of war as he could, so he also booked a ticket on a ship heading to the land Down Under. There they were in the great Southern land and they both ended up in Brisbane. My parents met at a naturalisation ceremony at Brisbane City Hall. The song, 'Some enchanted evening,' was playing; their eyes met across a crowded room, they fell in love and were engaged and married within two weeks – very romantic. Both were 40 at that time, and they didn't think it was possible for them to have a child. For the first six months of her pregnancy, Mama thought I was the change of life. She didn't think that she could possibly be pregnant, but she was, and I arrived full of the joys and juices of life, was treated like a miracle baby, and spoiled rotten.

I had several health challenges as a baby and as a young child, and nearly died a few times from one thing or another. At the age of four, I had a major operation on my leg that saw me hospitalised for months and in plaster for nearly a year, then having to learn to walk all over again. Of course, I didn't realise I was so ill, and it was much harder on my poor parents who thought their miracle baby was going to be snatched away from them several times. Poor darlings. Both my parents had lovely singing voices, and I've sung all my life too. My favourite song as a child was, 'Jesus wants me for a sunbeam.' A few years ago, I did a workshop aimed at finding one's purpose in life. It took me back to my childhood to find what I really loved the most. I have to say, I haven't found a better raison d'etre than the theme of that childhood song. Hopefully I succeed sometimes.

Brisbane in the 1950s was a cultural backwater. Tired of being tagged a BNAB – 'bloody new Australian bastard,' Papa was only too happy to go along with Mama's gypsy heart and head to the outback for adventure and a taste of the real Australia. My brother had run away from college to the outback not long before, and we'd received a letter from a cattle station owner saying that Des was at their property and they thought he was a good lad, and were training him to be a head stockman. Naturally, that also drew us to the outback where the earth was red and dry, and the sky was the colour of Jacaranda trees in bloom. I have a distinct memory of lying on the ground and squinting my eyes till the blossoms blended into the sky. Brolgas would come every year to our place and do their wonderful courtship dances; kangaroos, wallabies, koalas and goannas were everywhere. My parents got work first of all, on a sheep station called Alroy, north-west of Longreach. But after a couple of tough years of drought, and Mama facing challenges with brown snakes coming up through the floorboards into the kitchen every day looking for relief from the heat, they moved to the town of Longreach itself, where we lived until I was 12. It didn't rain for seven years when we were out there, and I remember the day it finally rained; children who had never seen rain were running around completely freaked out by the water pouring from the sky. Mama got a job with 4LG, the local radio station whose transmitter was out of town next to the Thompson River and an Aboriginal mission. I grew up with the Aboriginal kids as my playmates, and we had fun playing in the dry Thompson River bed. I am so grateful for those experiences out west.

When I was nine, a new Gospel Chapel came to Longreach, and Mama convinced Dad that we should go check it out. The evangelist gave a moving sermon calling us home to God's heart, and asked people to come down to the front of the church if they wanted to be reborn in Christ. I thought, "Yes!" So I jumped up and headed down the aisle. Mama told me that she and Papa looked at each other with surprise, smiled, shrugged and then followed me down the aisle to be baptised and born again in Jesus. All for one and one for all, we were the three musketeers. I went home that night and was overwhelmed by a feeling of love and joy. I was in my bedroom and prayed, "Please dear Jesus, give me a sign that you're with me." It was a very calm night, but at that moment, the curtains alongside my windows blew open gently and a sweet zephyr breeze came through the window and blew over me. I felt Jesus' heart, and I knew it was my sign. So began a five-year journey with the Gospel Chapel. I joined the 'Every Girl's Rally,' (youth group) and was quite the little evangelist, witnessing at every opportunity to earn those stars for my heavenly crown.

Mama's gypsy gene kicked in again around then, and we decided to travel from the red-hot outback to the cold and wet island of Tasmania. We connected with the Burnie Chapter of our church where the father of our Longreach pastor lived. We rented a house that overlooked the Burnie Harbour. On one side of us lived a family with a little Australian Terrier dog, and on the other side, lived a bagpipe player. When the bagpipe player would start playing, the little dog would start howling, and we would always laugh at the crazy symphony that ensued. So it was a wild and atmospheric year in a rather Wuthering Heights sort of way. But we decided it was a bit too moist and interesting down there, and we moved back to sunny Queensland after a year in Brisbane. Here, I completed high school at Kelvin Grove, and then went on to attend Queensland University at the St Lucia Campus where I did an Arts degree with an English major.

Loving singing and music as I did, I was in every school show, choir and musical group possible throughout my school life. When I left university, I started working in film and television. I got a job working as a production assistant on a couple of television shows, national children's TV shows (The Saturday show and Kindy) and, at the same time, kept the musical side going by singing in rock bands, rock musicals, big bands and stage shows. When I was doing a rock musical version of Macbeth, and we'd been rehearsing and rehearsing, and I'd been dancing and singing for hours, out of the blue, I had a very visceral, mystical experience that swept over me. I think I must have somehow connected with God's heart, because I knew beyond any doubt, that everything was so wonderfully perfectly alright, and that any of the things we worry about in life didn't matter a jot. It was such a powerful experience, I can only describe it as a mind, body, soul orgasm. Pure bliss. I have never forgotten it.

Even though life was taking me away from strict church experiences, thankfully my spiritual journey continued. God was in my heart, and nothing was going to change that. This spirituality came from every angle: the Bible, The Tibetan book of living and dying, the Bhagavad Gita, the Koran, Confucianism, Ancient Japanese Shinto religion, Buddhism, Hinduism, Carlos Castaneda, Herman Hesse, Descartes, Nietzsche, Native American spirituality, Aboriginal Dreamtime legends, and even Lobsang Rampa, Alistair Crowley and the dark arts. I was thirsty for all things arcane. I experimented with mind-altering drugs too, and thank God I came through that relatively unscathed. The drugs certainly broadened my mind, and I can understand why various cultures use them as a tool for spiritual growth. I learnt transcendental meditation and other meditation techniques, and found them very helpful practical tools to rest my mind and promote peace within myself. I also love chanting. I joined Muktananda's Ashram, and remember one memorable time I went there to chant. Chanting took me out of my body and into the cosmos. When I finished chanting, I thought two or three hours had passed, but in fact it was seven hours. When I walked out of the Ashram, I felt I was literally walking a foot off the ground, and this stayed with me for days. I can recommend chanting if you want to lift your spirit. My career in film and television forged ahead, where I worked in production and post-production on shows such as Cop shop, Holiday island, Skyways, Mission impossible, and also as a casting director for many award-winning TV commercials.

Being Irish, my mother was full of magical stories that inspired my childhood. Leprechauns, pixies and fairies all seemed quite normal and real to me. Mama also had mystical experiences. Her older sister had passed at 13 years of age. One evening when Mama was about ten, she was late getting home for dinner and decided to take a shortcut through the park. Just as she was about to enter the park, her dead sister appeared to her and told her not to go through the park but to go home the long way. Worried that her mother would be angry with her for being late, she objected. But her sister convinced her to go the long way. Next morning came the news that someone had been murdered in the park at the time she was going to be taking her 'shortcut.' My grandmother didn't believe Mama and had been angry the night before. However, in the morning, she was in a flood of tears on her knees giving thanks to God for Mama's deliverance. Another time, when my grandmother was dying, the nurse who was helping to care for her in the family home, told Mama to have a break and that she'd call her if anything changed. As Mama lay on her bed, her father, who had passed a few years earlier, appeared at the foot of her bed and said, "Don't worry lassie, I'll look after your mother now." Mama jumped up, and as she ran into the hall, the nurse was coming out of the door of her mother's room to tell her that her mother was passing. My father was a both feet on the ground type of man and eschewed such airy-fairy ideas. He had no time for mysticism and was more interested in science and practical knowledge. I have always found myself trying to balance these two sides of my nature. As it happens, since coming to the Family Federation for World Peace and Unification (FFWPU) and studying the Divine Principle, I now understand that both science and religion play a vital part in informing our inner and outer intelligence. Both science and religion are needed if we are to step into our wholeness as true children of God who are capable of fostering peace on earth, which is another term for heaven on earth.

My father lost a leg to diabetes and lost his life to the disease in 1979. Mama was devastated by his passing because they had been inseparable and had never spent a night apart. Their love had only deepened as the years passed, and for a while, I wondered how she was going to survive such a loss. A nice moment occurred at the funeral parlour as we were saying our goodbyes to him. We were kissing him and sobbing, when over the loudspeakers came their song, 'Some enchanted evening.' What a panacea that was, especially for Mama. Mama had major health challenges too, but somehow she kept rallying and lived a further nine years after Dad died. She attended many personal development workshops with me during those years, and I loved how she was forever young that way, open to new ideas and incorporating them into her spiritual mandala. At the end of her life, she lived at Caritas Christi Hospice in Kew, Melbourne. In a lovely last little bit of magic, the priest at the Hospice turned out to be Irish, and indeed, was from Mama's parish in Belfast, Carrick Fergus. She was able to spend her last months in his spiritual care, which brought her great peace and joy. Also, in true Patsy style, her passing was full of magic and grace. She had been rather 'out of it' due to the administered drugs, when suddenly out of the blue, she sat bolt upright in bed, gripped my hand firmly, grinning broadly and turned to me. Her eyes were as bright and cognisant as I had ever seen them, and she was totally with it again. Then, still grinning broadly, she turned to look into the distance and off she went. She had always promised me that if there was a way to let me know what lay beyond this life she would, and I believe in that moment SHE DID. Not long after Mama passed in 1988, I had a relationship with a Polish photographer who was also a scientist. When I told him the story of Mama's passing, he gave me the scientific 'cascading brain chemicals' explanation of her experience and it really sent me into a dark night of the soul. His 'scientific' explanation made sense, and his lambasting of anything spiritual really affected me deeply, probably because I loved him and my heart was torn between him and everything that my life to date had brought to my soul. We were together for five years, and I spent that time in a new career as a fashion and beauty photographer. I adored photography and may well have stayed in that career had the relationship not ended.

However, it did end, and I loaded up my old Ford wagon with as many of my things as I could, including my dog, Zashi, and my cat, Mexico, and headed up the highway to Byron Bay and new adventures. We looked rather like the Beverley Hillbillies when they loaded up the truck and headed to Beverley Hills that is. Byron Bay is the most easterly point of Australia, incredibly beautiful, and deeply healing. It is a sacred Aboriginal place where the Rainbow Serpent returned into the sea, having completed the creation of Australia. Every day I swam in the ocean feeling years of stress and trauma being washed away. Every day I was in tears of gratitude for being brought to this heavenly place. I didn't know anything much about the place before going there, I just had a strong feeling to go. I ended up doing a popular magazine style radio show on 99.9 Bay FM for ten years, getting involved in all sorts of community service, and loving every moment of my time. I had just turned 40 and to my surprise, realised that my life really was just beginning all over again. I meditated, swam, rode my pushbike everywhere, did yoga, dyed my hair turquoise-blue, grew dreadlocks, danced all night at rave parties in the hills around Byron and on the beaches, and did a lot of singing in stage shows and cabarets. I also hosted youth festivals and New Year's events in the town centre, emceed community trivia nights, and really got my mojo and my spiritual faith back again. Hallelujah.

In 1999, I attended the Woodford Folk Festival where I ran into an old friend who had written a lot of the rock musicals I'd done in the 70s. We reconnected in a great way, and through her I met my first boyfriend again. Robert and I enjoyed the next eight years together. He wasn't well, and I was as much a caregiver as a partner. However, through our relationship, he reconnected with his art, being a great artist himself. He had been married and had a beautiful daughter, Bianca, who is still very dear to me. Robbie did some of his best art during our time together, and I felt privileged to be there for him during his victorious battle against alcoholism and his valiant fight against the oesophageal cancer that claimed his life in 2007. When he passed, I decided to return to Victoria. Spending time with family was very soothing, and I also spent a year looking after a dear friend's country property at Clydesdale near Daylesford. I grew my first vegie garden, and landscaped her garden with the beautiful granite rocks that work their way up to the surface in that old gold mining country. I also made a fairy garden for her daughter, which reconnected me with all the Irish, fairy magic of my childhood; it was one of the most fun things I've ever done. Daylesford is rather like the Byron Bay of the south, and I met a dear old friend there who I hadn't seen for over 30 years. She is a Buddhist, and I must credit her for really helping me move through the grief of Robbie's passing. I spent another year or so looking after the five-year old daughter of a dear, Jewish friend in Caulfield, Melbourne; oh, what a joy that was. Her grandmother had been one of my dearest friends, and I happily told her many stories about the grandma she had never known. It was wonderful and healing to be around children again, after years of caring for the sick and dying.

My time in Bryon Bay had reignited my spirituality. So when I met a God-centred man online who was living off the grid in New Mexico by using solar power and living in a simple, honest way, I was open and ready for the next steps on my spiritual path. Teddy is three-quarter African American, and one-quarter Native American. He had been brought up a Christian, and has always had a very strong faith. When he was quite young, he set off from home on a spiritual quest, and not long into his journey, he came upon the Divine Principle, so passionately taught by Rev. Dr. Sun Myung Moon. He joined the FFWPU in the late 70s. Teddy has the gift of prophecy, and was totally inspired by the teaching of the FFWPU and Rev. Moon. So he travelled the country preaching and doing lots of things with the church, including helping to restore and plaster the New Yorker Hotel. He was even jailed for street preaching during those years. I was so grateful to have, at last, met a man with whom I could share my love for God, and who was living a spiritual path. That was always missing in my previous relationships, and had been a big bone of contention. At first, when he told me he was a 'Moonie,' I was a bit shocked. There is so much bad press about Rev. Moon out there, and my research abilities, which were honed in the film industry, found every single scandalous one ever printed. Luckily I found lots of other information which informed a more balanced view of Rev. Moon. I was quickly aware of the agendas of the people who were responsible for the slander, and felt full admiration for how Rev. Moon had carried on with his mission, despite the controversy that raged around and about him.

After a few months of communicating with Teddy online, and after reading Rev. Moon's writings, I joined the Melbourne FFWPU. I came to understand that Father Moon loved Jesus even more than I did, and I learnt of the sacrifices he had made to continue Jesus' mission. To my last breath, I came to love him and to feel committed to helping restore God's providence and God's original plan for mankind. When I was still unsure of this path, I was praying a lot and meditating for divine guidance, and it came to me in meditation one day, "By their deeds ye shall know them." In truth, I have never met a group of people whose hearts and deeds are so beautifully pure and selfless.

I had smoked marijuana pretty much daily since I was about 19 years old. Even though other drugs came and went, marijuana was a constant stress reliever in my life. I wasn't fond of alcohol, but I loved the herb. I preferred it to the antidepressant drugs I was prescribed upon being diagnosed with post-traumatic stress and depression after caring for my folks and Robbie during their illnesses. In Robbie's case, I was his sole carer, and for the last two years of his life, I hardly slept at all; it was very stressful and exhausting. When I started to get the spiritual nourishment I was really looking for from the Divine Principle, I was able to give up my reliance on marijuana. This not only surprised me, but also surprised everyone who knew me; they thought I would never be able to give it up. This is my personal experience of how the Divine Principle has changed my life. I am growing in my love for, and dedication to this course.

I am not a financially wealthy person and neither is Teddy. However, we are committed to being together. I visited him for three months in 2013, and will be going again in April 2016 for another three months. Life off the grid is rather like living in a Third World country. There is no electricity, no running water, no fridge, no stove, no corner shop to pick up some yummy treat, and none of the comforts of home. Yikes! Could this old dog really learn these new tricks? It's a 4,267-metre high desert mesa; hot as Hades during the day, but blessedly cool at night. The only thing that grows there is sage bush, and keeping warm in the snowy winters is a real challenge too. It is, however, very beautiful, being surrounded by the magnificent Sangre de Cristo Mountain Range which are snow-capped most of the year. The region is a mix of Native American, Spanish and American cultures. The predominant architecture is adobe, fashioned into wonderfully creative shapes. Many movies have been shot in the area, for example, Easy rider and Back to the future. For many years, famous artists like Georgia O'Keefe and D.H Lawrence have flocked to the area for the inspiration that can come from the dramatic landscape and sense of freedom in the air. Mabel Dodge Luhan, a wealthy American patron of the arts, settled there. She married a local Tiwa Indian man named Tony Luhan, and built an incredible home that Dennis Hopper bought from them in the 70s. It is open to the public now, and I dreamt of moving in there; dream on Barbie, lol. Julia Roberts was also a famous resident of the area. There are many artists and musicians living there who have chosen to leave the stress of city life behind, and be self-sufficient and free. The Rio Grande River has cut a mile-deep canyon through the mesa, and the climb down the gorge to the actual river is rewarded by a heavenly soak in steamy hot springs next to the river; it gives one's body a rainbow halo from the minerals in the water and it is very beautiful. Teddy has built himself a home that looks like a dragonfly when the windows are opened. There are many interesting hand built homes and environmentally friendly 'earth ships.' We are planning to build a round, rammed earth home to accommodate us both. Many people come to the area in search of Utopia, however, it is not an easy place to survive in. Dotted around the mesa are the cars and half built houses of those who found the going too tough. I lost 30 pounds the first two months I was there just doing what had to be done every day to survive. If I wanted water for washing up or a shower, I would go downstairs to the barrel we'd carted from a well located miles away, syphon some out with a hose into a bucket, carry that upstairs, pour it into a big pot, heat that on the barbeque, carry that back downstairs to the rather ingenious shower Teddy has made, climb onto a chair and lift the pot up and pour it into a plastic container above the shower. Everything takes effort, and you really have to go with the flow and just tackle whatever presents itself each day. This may be repairing the solar panels that got damaged in the late afternoon storm, or the high wind that swept through the afternoon or evening; or trekking into Taos itself, which is about 25 miles away to get water, because a coyote knocked over the water barrel during the night. There is no work as such. Teddy, who is a qualified carpenter and builder, is working hard teaching himself 3D computer graphics so that he can make a living from art and illustrations. That is coming along well, although most of his clients have been mesa residents who use barter products to pay for a CD cover he might design, or for promotional material he might produce. I'm also working on my own art, writing and drawing children's book illustrations, hoping it will be a new career path for me too. While it seems a very big hill to climb to gather all the funds Teddy and I need for immigration costs, wedding and blessing fees etc. I have faith that we WILL be together, and that we will find a sponsor. Every day that passes shows me how much I needed to learn before our relationship could really blossom, so I am only grateful for the time it is taking for us to come together and to be 'blessed.' God's timing, not ours!

I joined the Women's Federation for World Peace (WFWP) a couple of years ago, and am currently the Victorian Vice-President and loving being part of such an inspiring group of women that encompasses all ages, cultures and religions. They are doing such good work in both the Pacific Islands and here in Australia. Recently, we have had an influx of inspiring young women onto our Board, which is going to take us to a whole new level of excellence and effectiveness; it's most exciting.

When I move to New Mexico, I have every faith that I will be able to continue the work of WFWP over there; many women of real substance are already doing great work for the Tiwa Indian Nation, and for other groups and individuals in the community.

Thank you for the opportunity to share 'my story' with you.

Naya's Hungarian Chicken

Serves 4-6

INGREDIENTS

3 tbsp sweet Hungarian paprika
1 cup plain wholemeal flour
1 to 1½ kg whole chicken, cut into pieces
2 tbsp coconut oil
1 tbsp butter
Pink Himalayan salt and ground black pepper, to taste. (Be generous with the pepper.)
4 cloves fresh garlic
1 cup diced brown onion
1 leek
1 cup white wine
1 cup chicken stock
Small can chopped roma tomatoes
roughly chopped European parsley
½ - 1 cup sour cream or pure cream
1 cup basmati rice
Good sized handful baby spinach leaves

METHOD

1. Mix 1 tablespoon of the sweet paprika through the flour and coat the chicken pieces.
2. In a heavy deep sided pan heat the coconut oil and butter and brown chicken on all sides. Season the chicken with salt and pepper. Remove chicken and set aside.
3. Add the onion, garlic and the leek to the frypan. Cook until just tender, but not brown. Stir in other 2 tablespoons sweet paprika.
4. Return the chicken to frypan, turn the chicken to coat the pieces with the paprika/onion/garlic/leek mixture. Add the wine, stock and the tomatoes.
5. Bring to a boil; then reduce the heat, cover and simmer for an hour or so until the chicken is fully cooked and tender.
6. Stir in the sour cream or pure cream. Heat through and toss the European parsley on top of the meal so that the heat of the chicken just wilts the parsley slightly.
7. Cook the rice in a steamer and when cooked mix through the baby spinach leaves.
8. Serve the Hungarian chicken on top of the rice/spinach mix and ENJOY.

Zakia Baig - The unheard story

Hello everybody, good afternoon. Thank you for having me. I feel privileged to be among this group of very inspirational ladies. I always say, let us come together, then we can always do more things.

My name is Zakia Baig. I am a Shia Muslim from Pakistan and belong to the Hazara people. I was born in Pakistan, but my grandfather originated from Afghanistan. Hazarus people look slightly Chinese and originate from Afghanistan. We are a mixture of Turkish and Mongolian, and were Buddhist before we began to follow the Islamic faith tradition. Close to 2,000 years ago, the Hazara people carved huge Buddha monuments into the Afghanistan mountains. The largest monuments were destroyed in 2004 by the Taliban. It does not matter what belief we have; one religion or one faith cannot categorise someone as a good person or a bad person. We are all human; there is no difference between a person's colour, faith or caste.

I was born as the first child of my parents. At that time, Pakistan did not exist; it was only India. My father was not Pakistan at that time; he was Indian. He was born in what is now Pakistan and was raised by a very modest family; his parents were labourers. My father always loved education and he was a sports person. When I was born, he said that he loved daughters. After me, there were four sons. There was no daughter again, so my father brought me up like a son. He always encouraged me saying, "Do not feel inferior." But, in our culture, daughters were always punished. The daughters have to always be waiting on, and taking care of their brothers. People would say to the girls, "Do not worry about your food, but your brother should have food." That kind of behaviour was in our culture. But, my father always encouraged me, and I thank God for giving me that kind of father. My father said to me, "You are not a girl; get an education and go high. No matter what comes, do not sell fish, because you know you can find money, you can find comfort, but you cannot find peace and fulfilment unless you help people." At the start of year 11, I had the chance to work with an organisation helping students who were Hazara refugees from Afghanistan. In south-east Pakistan in the Quetta region, there are 400,000 to 600,000 Hazara people living as refugees from Afghanistan.

In 1919, 62 per cent of the Hazara population in Afghanistan were massacred and many of the remaining people fled as refugees into the Quetta region of India, now Pakistan. From 1979, the Soviet Union controlled Afghanistan and killed many people, including the Hazara people who fought for the state. Once again, the Hazara took refuge in Pakistan. Then, again, there was a war among the Afghanistan tribes, and the Hazara people were heavily targeted. The people escaped and went into Quetta, Pakistan, and other countries. In 1998, the Taliban came and indiscriminately killed 4,000 to 6,000 Hazara people through ethnic cleansing. Hazaras were told that there was no room for them in Afghanistan and if they have a place to go, it is only to the graveyards. Uzbek people live in Uzbekistan, and Tajik people live in Tajikistan. However, Hazara people were told that they have no country, even though Afghanistan is the historical origin of the Hazara people; they are the indigenous population.

My family was living in Quetta, Pakistan, a city of refugees. As a teenager, I opened my eyes and started seeing chaos all around me. There was an imbalance of gender, with many widows, elderly and children in all kind of need. When there is war or conflict, it is the children and women who suffer more than men. As a young girl, that put me in a situation where I decided not to stay at home. But my culture did not allow girls to join boys in the workforce. It was my father who pushed me and encouraged me to hurry up and go. My father said that we need people who can give others a hand; he encouraged me to bring a change to society. From a very young age, he is the reason why I wanted change. I did not like it when my Mom used to say, "You are a girl, you don't deserve to be like your brothers." I wanted to teach my mother and other women that children are all the same, no matter what their gender. I started working for girls' rights by writing, playing in dramas and speaking out from a very young age. After I completed my studies, I worked in a not-for-profit community school as a primary school teacher.

I loved encouraging girls. When they cried, I cried with them. I said, "Come on, just wipe off your tears. It is now your day and you can go, you can do it." I did everything to encourage women, especially the young girls, by encouraging them to gain their power, their energy and not to go down. I used to write in a community magazine about women's rights; equality,

equality and equality. There is nothing more important than equality; it is not a small thing. We have to treat each other equal, as good human beings.

My future husband read my writing in the magazine. When it was time for him to marry, he asked his mother to go and ask Zakia's hand saying, "This is the girl that I want for my life and to be the mother of my children." We never met each other and we had never talked to each other, so when he asked for my hand I said, "Why this man? He must come here. I do not know him." My brothers told me that he is my kind of person and that he is a good man. This was the way we got married. My husband was also a teacher, a professor.

My first son became very sick with leukaemia, but there were no good hospitals in Quetta city. We had to take our very sick four-year-old son to the inner city for medication and chemotherapy. I took him again and again and again to Quetta city, trying to help him understand we need to go to hospital. This is what gave me the mother's power to change and work for my son. Together, we went to the hospitals and did all the chemotherapy. I used to hold my son in the hospital. It was very painful for me, but I can say that I discovered God in my body and I always talked to my God. Our son survived some months, but could not continue living. There is something around us and inside us that gives us the strength and power to change things in our lives.

Soon after, I established an organisation to help ladies in Pakistan, because there were many widows and orphans who fled after the ethnic cleansing by the Taliban in Afghanistan. When I saw the widows and orphans begging, it was unbearable for me. The women were still young, they were asking for a job, but there were no jobs. They had children; we had to give them money and this was the way my husband and I helped them. My husband left teaching and started his own business; it was a good business. I said to him, "Let's do something for them. We should teach them skills so they can earn money for themselves." We established a skill centre on the first floor of our home; it ran for three years. We taught 200 women, girls and boys to study English and gain skills in computing, sewing and embroidery. There were no male adult students, because the ladies felt more comfortable that way.

But again, bad energy comes around, negative energy; people who do not like you, people who do not allow girls to find themselves. So one day, a man came to me and said, "I am a journalist and I want to interview you about what you are doing." I told him that we are empowering ladies to earn money for themselves, raise their children and with this, gain respect within their homes. When women get respect inside their home, they can raise their children well and they can be happy. This was our motivation; we should start this kind of thing. The journalist asked, "Why teach them English? English is not your language. Why are you teaching them computers? They do not need a computer. So what are you really selling here, and why are you teaching them?" He accused me of being an agent sent from somewhere and said that the ladies should be taught religion, their own language and their responsibilities at home. I told the journalist that we are living in a global village. These women can get energy from all around the world. They should feel valuable to themselves. They should be empowered by sources outside of their home. One day, I got a phone call from the local police and they questioned me as to what I was doing. I told them that I am just running a skill centre for ladies. They said, "You are in danger, you are in danger, what do you want us to do for you? Do you want our employees to stand at your door and give security to you and your girls coming to your centre?" I replied, "If you bring your security guards to my doors, no-one will come." So I moved the education centre into the community. We received threats and feared that somebody would come into the centre and harm the students and teachers. Therefore, we decided to leave Pakistan. I was still young, so my husband encouraged me to go to Australia as a student rather than leaving by boat as a refugee, which is dangerous for all of us.

I came to Australia as a student and did hospitality management. After graduating, when I went for job interviews, nobody gave me a position. Finally, I decided to buy a coffee shop franchise that was for sale, and my husband sent me the money. I asked the owner, "Are you giving me a job?" He said, "No, he cannot." I said, "Are you selling me your shop?" He said, "Yes, yes." Finally, the franchise managers asked me, "Can you run this?" I replied, "Yes I can. I have done the hospitality course. I know I can run the business." The reply back was, "No, we cannot sell the shop to you, even if you give us the money. You are from Pakistan and you do not have experience." I insisted, "Let us do it. Sell me the shop. I can do it." He said, "Oh Zakia, you have no experience. You know our company is famous. We could lose all our customers." Then I brought my daughter into the negotiation to buy the shop. Finally, the owner said, "All right, we will give you a chance to try it out." I gave my money as a deposit and I took over the management of the shop. My daughter was 18 and my son was 16. Twelve of us worked in the coffee shop; myself, my daughter, my sister and her husband and some Chinese girls and boys. I was wearing the uniform and cap. I did the accounts, the stock, the baking, the cleaning and there was a time when I even made coffee. Nothing was impossible. One Thursday, the shop was really overcrowded and we were having a line of customers waiting for our coffee. Suddenly the franchise manager appeared and said, "Zakia, can we talk to you outside?" Three men had come from

Sydney to watch me; they were surprised to see me making coffee. I said, "I can do everything, I can do anything. This shop was running at a loss and I increased its sales by ten per cent." I told them, "You cannot judge people by their scarves, by their colour. The person is inside. Give them the opportunity, then you will know what capabilities they have. It does not matter what colour, what religion, what background people have. It is just a matter of giving people encouragement and an opportunity." The men said, "My God you are incredible. You are different, you are different." I then told the managers, "Remember when you wouldn't sell this shop to me. Well, I am not buying it. It is not worth it; I am your slave. While working here, I am making no profit, because you get all money." Then the managers offered to reduce the buying cost of this store or manage another branch; they even offered me a branch in Canberra.

A not-for-profit organisation encouraged me to enter into a national competition to tell my 90-second story about how my community matters in Australia. My daughter took her mobile phone and I told the story. We checked the time. We trained and timed again and again until the story fit into 90 seconds. Oh my God, I won it! It was unbelievable. On Australia Day, my daughter and I were given a chance to meet the Prime Minister in Canberra; it was breathtaking. We were sponsored to travel to Canberra for a few days; everything was taken care of, everything was free. The 90-second story was about 'my people are in danger.' Hazarus are in danger, and you can do something for them. Raise a voice and be our voice. We need people like you. This country has given me a lot of courage; it is a country of peace and equal opportunity. This country is a women's country; we never had such opportunities that we have here. We just have to decide, then go and grab an opportunity. From this prize, I was on YouTube and national TV everywhere. This organisation also encouraged me to apply for a scholarship to the UN in Geneva. I put my application in, did a telephone interview, and received the scholarship to study minority rights at the United Nations for five months. I did all the assignments and got a chance to speak for three minutes at the United Nations Council on minority rights. I submitted recommendations about the rights of the Hazara community in Pakistan and Afghanistan, and how to deal with the situation.

These are the things that we have to consider. Thank you.

Chicken or Lamb Biryani - from Khana Khazana

A rich mix of strong Indian spices and lamb or beef chunks that are sautéed in spices, makes this rice variant a favourite with the carnivore population.

Serves 4-6

INGREDIENTS

Chicken or lamb on the bone cut into 4cm pieces
500g Sela (ukda) **basmati rice, soaked**
1 ½ **cup ginger paste**
1 tbsp garlic paste
1 tbsp green chilli paste
1 tbsp coriander (dhania) **powder**
1 tbsp roasted cumin (bhuna jeera) **powder**
1 tbsp garam masala powder
1 tsp green cardamom (chhoti elaichi) **powder**
1 tsp salt to taste
Yogurt (dahi)
1 cup oil
3 tablespoons bay leaf powder

1 clove
4 **green cardamoms** (chhoti elaichi)
2 **black cardamoms** (badi elaichi)
1 cup of chicken stock
5 cups milk
A few **saffron threads** (kesar)
1 tbsp **caraway seeds** (shahi jeera)
1 tsp ginger powder
2cm ginger piece, cut into thin strips
Onions sliced and deep fried
2 medium **fresh mint leaves** (pudina) chopped
½ **cup fresh coriander leaves** (hara dhania) **chopped**
2 tablespoons Kewra water
1 teaspoon rose water

Method on next page.

Chicken or Lamb Biryani - from Khana Khazana

METHOD

1. Marinate the chicken in a mixture of ginger paste, garlic paste, green chilli paste, coriander powder, cumin powder, garam masala powder, cardamom powder, salt and yogurt for about half an hour.
2. Heat one tablespoon oil in a pan. Add the bay leaf, cloves, green cardamoms and black cardamom and sauté for half a minute. Add the rice and sauté for a minute. Add the chicken stock and bring to a boil. Lower the heat and cook for eight to ten minutes or till the rice is three fourth done. Drain and set aside.
3. Soak saffron in the milk.
4. Heat the remaining oil in a thick-bottomed pan. Add the caraway seeds and sauté till fragrant. Add the marinated chicken and sauté for three to four minutes or till it is half cooked.
5. Remove the pan from the heat. Spread the rice over the chicken. Sprinkle saffron flavoured milk, ginger strips, fried onions, chopped fresh mint and coriander, kewra water and rose water over the rice. Cover and cook for fifteen to twenty minutes over low heat.
6. Serve hot with a raita of your choice.

Jenny Funston - Journey to Japan

I am the coordinator of all the Byakko and Peace Prayer Society activities throughout the countries of Oceania, but my spiritual background is Anglican. My parents sent us to Sunday school and church until I moved from New South Wales to Victoria. In Victoria, we lived on a farm so we weren't living close to a church. We lived on the land on a dairy farm very close to nature, and that was always really, really beautiful. Wandering down to the creek and finding a platypus – we always loved that.

When I went to university, I met my husband, Steve, through the Evangelical Union. It was a Christian group where we participated in activities. I'm a bit of a mix and I've become even more of a mix spiritually as time has gone on. My husband was a Presbyterian. Later, we both started going to a Baptist Church and got baptised. I'd had the Anglican baptism with water splashed on the top of my head, but in the Baptist Church, baptism means full water immersion.

I had always wanted to be a primary school teacher. However, when I started, primary school teachers attended a teacher's college. If you went to university, you came out as a secondary school teacher only. My teachers encouraged me to go to university; so that's where I met my husband. At the end of first year, I failed two of my four subjects. I went to the Education Ministry and said, "I really want to do primary school teaching." The man who interviewed me was not the kindest of men and said gruffly, "Why do you think we should give you a second chance and let you go to primary school teacher training instead?" This wasn't the answer I gave him, but the answer I got inside was, "Because this is what God wants me to do. This is my path." I had wanted to be a primary school teacher ever since I was in grade two. In the end, I was allowed to switch over to primary school teaching and was penalised a term's studentship; but that was fine. When my husband and

54

I left university, my husband moved right away from formal religion and became interested in a group that was a mixture of people.

We attended some of that during a time when we lived in Adelaide. We had two children, and life just rolled along. However, I had more awareness of what God meant in my life. I can remember many days when I was thinking about God and God's love. You hear so many stories from people about what God is and what love is. I thought God must love everyone and everything, because I could love my husband and when I had a child, I did not half the love. The love expanded to encompass them both. When I had my second child, the love did not go down to a third, it just expanded. I thought, "If I can feel that as a human, then God must be something just absolutely extraordinary."

When my children were young, there were big turning points in my life about what God was; there was always an exploration with ups and downs, but always a constant search. As an adult, I can remember my father saying to me, "Jenny, one of the things about you is that no matter what happens, even as a child, if we would growl at you, you would always go away and think about it, look for all the different facets and all the different sides of things. You're still doing the same thing as an adult." My father could see that I was searching. For instance, I studied Reiki and other healing modalities which were also ways that I connected to what I might call our Source, or God. I don't mind what words people use; certainly I can use the word God, but I will also use Source, Universal Light or love. It doesn't really matter because there are so many words that people use.

I can remember a particular book that I gave to a friend of my mother. The book explored, "I am God," meaning I have God's essence of love and compassion. She said, "Jenny I don't know whether I can look at it like that." I said, "Well, do you think that you are loved? Can you say I am loved?" She said, "Oh yes, yes. I can say I am loved." I replied, "Well, just change the words. It doesn't really matter. Feel what's inside your heart that makes you feel comfortable, that makes you want to smile." Be compassionate, laugh, have fun.

As time went on, there was more and more of a search for something that was still incomplete within myself. I was happy enough; I went back into teaching, and when my kids were in late primary school, I went back to full-time primary school teaching for a few years. Then I left and I started to work with a Japanese organisation part-time. Students would come from Japan, and we organised 'home stay' with Japanese students staying with an Australian family. In 1996, I had the opportunity to go to Japan and stay with a family. They didn't know English, and I didn't know Japanese. The Japanese family used an electronic dictionary, and I had the most marvellous time. I felt as though I had gone home, which was an interesting experience when you go into another culture and the food all seems familiar – it all seemed normal.

Because I believe in reincarnation, I believe that as a spirit, I've lived forever and this lifetime is just Jenny Funston's costume, learning about love. One day in 1997, I went to the library and a book moved out of the bookshelf; it was about the Byakko Shinko Kai and the Peace Prayer Society; it moved a centimetre in front of me; it just went boing! Okay, I thought, "Let's pick that one up." I can still remember; I stood in front of the bookcase and gleaned through the book and thought, "Oh, this is the same as A course in miracles," which I have also studied and which I love. The philosophy of Byakko Shinko Kai still has the basis of Christianity, a system of love; love thy neighbour as thyself. I read the book and loved it. The philosophy felt close to my heart. I felt so grateful, that I wrote a hand written thank you letter to the publisher. I can remember getting some paper with an Australian design, little koalas and kangaroos all around the edge. A few weeks later, I received a letter back from an editor who looks after all the English publications for the author. It made a huge impact; I started receiving English publications that had been translated from Japanese into English. As I read, I thought, "Oh, the soul's singing, absolutely singing." I had my basic Christian belief, but my life experiences had expanded my concept of what God was. We are all part of a 'oneness,' and this organisation for me really sat beautifully with that.

In 1998, I won a trip to Japan. I had been working with the exchange program and the organisation decided they would have another Japanese trip. The names of group leaders like myself and host families were put in a hat for a lucky draw. I won one of three trips from Australia! So I had another experience of home stay in Japan. Lovely, I love Japan. I think I was Japanese somewhere along the line in a past lifetime. The English editor, Mary, offered to take me to visit the Byakko Shinko Kai Fuji Sanctuary and I thought, "Yes, yes please." It is located in the Asagiri plain on the foothills of Mount Fuji. Being from a family of dairy farmers in the countryside, I thought that it was really, really beautiful.

There's no accommodation for people at the Sanctuary, so they put me up in a hotel for four nights. What I experienced, I had never experienced anything like it, ever in my life. I didn't know much other than the organisation planted Peace Poles, used the prayer, 'May peace prevail on earth,' and believed that prayer is energy. At the Sanctuary was a huge round pyramid made of canvas. It's a high-energy centre. On one hill are seven stations used to facilitate people to let go of 'old baggage' step by step, and instead, feel gratitude to nature with infinite bright thoughts; such as infinite love, infinite happiness and infinite joy. The focus in moving through the stations is to change old habits.

People at the Sanctuary practice movements using sounds and breath called 'in.' The series of movements are based on sacred geometry, sound and breath. The energy that the movements generate is pretty awesome. I took a moment to go into a special place to make myself still and then stepped through the gate. It's an open gate with no fences on either side. I stepped across the gateway and all I could feel throughout my body was a strong, pulsating energy. I stood there and sobbed and sobbed and sobbed. I thought well, "I don't know what's going on here, but it's new." I can remember Mary saying to me, "You're very sensitive to energy." The pulsating energy stopped once I started moving again.

At the Sanctuary is an outdoor prayer field for people to sit in the prayer field. All prayer ceremonies are held outdoors; it doesn't matter whether there's snow, rain or hail. The main emphasis and focus of Byakko Shinko Kai is prayer energy-work. Individuals can then go out and join with organisations that might be doing hands-on work. Byakko Shinko Kai is hands-on prayer energy-work. We also do Flag Ceremonies where we honour every nation in the world. The perimeter of the prayer field is lined with flags of every nation, plus a United Nations flag. We send prayer blessings to each county. For us, when we use a country's flag, it's the spiritual essence of the country; everything that is positive. Twice a day, someone at the Sanctuary goes to the prayer field and prays for every country using the flags. Other members will also come and pray for every county, so often a prayer is delivered to each country more than twice a day, every day. Some of us also do the ceremony at home quite often. To reach the prayer field is a path of Peace Poles, with a Peace Pole for every country. The path of Peace Poles starts really wide and then gradually narrows. As soon as I stepped between the first two poles, the same pulsation in my body started and I thought, "Okay, alright. Here we go again." The pulsation stopped once I got right within the path. We walked up and approached the prayer field lined with flags. We stopped at the edge of the flag entrance and bowed to honour the energy field. Mary and I walked onto the prayer field, and all of a sudden, to my right, I felt a wall of very, very, wide energy. I don't know how to describe it other than energy. It wasn't pulsing this time; it felt like a wall of love, it just kept rolling, rolling and rolling over me. It was profound because I've read about people having experiences, but nothing like that had ever happened to me before. Once again I stood and cried. I'm a bit of a sook. All I could feel was love, just total 100 per cent love. I learnt a style of movement using sounds and breath, and met the spiritual chairwoman. She has three daughters who have now taken over her role. The staff explained to me that the 'work' has spiritual and physical components to it. I thought, "Well that's ruled me out," because I had a back that did this, and knees that did that, and I was then 47. I thought, "There's just no way I could do this physically." But the heart said, "Oh yes, yes I'm going to do that. I have to do that." Not in the sense of my ego having to, but my soul said, "I have to do this."

This was another turning point in my spiritual life. I left the Sanctuary and visited some Japanese friends. I had another week in Japan, and by the time I got home, I was really sick. I realise now that being at the Sanctuary had been a deep, deep cleansing; getting rid of lots and lots of things. It was December, and by February, I had filled in the forms to say, "Yes, I will do the program." But I couldn't work out how it was ever going to be achieved. My husband was a little bit anti; he wasn't sure about this. He'd always been a little bit afraid because I had always explored different faiths and traditions. I think he was afraid that I would join a sect or a cult and be taken away or something, and didn't understand that I was quite discerning. I probably did a very foolish thing. I didn't tell my husband anything much about my experiences in Japan or the program, because I just couldn't handle the 'who ha' from him, and I just didn't know what to say.

I began my activities. There were physical aspects with special 70-kilometre walks that had to be completed within two days. These were to stretch ourselves and prove to ourselves that we were capable of far more than we intellectually thought we could do, physically, mentally and emotionally. I've realised more in later years, what this training was about. To be honest, I was explained what the training does, but I don't think I fully comprehended. The training was to say, "Okay, just walk with the pain in your back or hips, or walk with joy." I did the training and the movement, sound and breath work that I had to do. But there was a catch as well; I had to complete the training at the Sanctuary and pay my own way to Japan. I didn't have any extra money at the time, and when I mentioned the idea to my husband, World War III almost erupted. I didn't know what to do. I was so encouraged by my adult children who typed a letter to their father to support me. My husband and I got to some agreement, but he still said, "We don't have the money."

I belonged to a little group called the Geelong Ladies of Wealth, where once a month, we would make some investments. We happened to have a meeting and a dinner two weeks before I was due to go, and one of my very close friends said, "You're going to Japan in two weeks," and I replied, "Well, no." So all the ladies joined in. "You've got to go; you've done all this training; you've got to go." I'm telling you these things because for my spiritual journey, this was a big leap of courage. I have fear barriers in myself, but looking back, I can see how I've grown by every challenge I've had to step into and move through. As time has gone by,

I've dropped more and more of the fear-base, and trusted more and more in the love and the God within me; the oneness, the joining and the support nourishes and nurtures me. When I came home from this meeting, I must have not looked very well and Steve asked me, "Are you alright?" I replied, "I'm just working out how I'm going to tell you I'm going to Japan in two weeks." He must have heard it, even though I garbled the sentence out. He went white and raced out of the room. So I'm sitting there, my stomach and heart going wobbly, and I thought, "Oh my goodness me." Steve came back into the room and sat down on the couch. This is another memory that still brings tears to my eyes; he looked at me and said, "Are you coming back?" He thought that a cult had got me and once I went to Japan, he'd never see me again. I thought, "Oh, the darling."

At eight o' clock in the morning, I got a phone call from the same friend who told me that I had to go to Japan. She said, "Jenny don't say anything, and please let me finish what I'm going to say to you now." I thought, "Oh, I've done something wrong. I must have offended somebody." "Jenny. I want to offer you the fare for you to travel to Japan. You can pay me back eventually. But if it takes years and years down the track, it doesn't matter. I want you to have that." I thought, "Okay." I had stepped into the idea and had created the opening for God to work. It was gifted to me in that moment because I had known in my heart that I needed to do this, and it was part of my mission in life; this is what I'd been born into this lifetime for. There was also a feeling in me that if I didn't go to Japan and do the training at this time, there wasn't any sense in being here. And I know this sounds really severe or tough. But the feeling to go was so strong, that my spiritual mission was to do 'my work' through this organisation. We all have our ways of doing things, and each one is as valid as the other and as beautiful as the other.

So yes. I went to Japan and finished my training in 1999. I climbed Mount Fuji, and I did that under special conditions also. In 2001, the organisation offered me the job of Oceania Coordinator. Still, a lot of my work is prayer work. But I also plant Peace Poles and do Flag Ceremonies. Sometimes, the Flag Ceremonies are only short. Sometimes we honour every nation where we name every nation and say, "May peace be in the Solomon Islands, or may peace be in Australia, may peace be in Afghanistan" etc. These are regular activities. We also do mandala writings where positive words are written in concentric circles. The words become an anchor; once they are written, that energy lives forever. In a spiritual sense, the energy continues to flow into the centre of the mandala and goes out horizontally. People can write special poems or something that they love; it might be a prayer from your faith. Anything that's positive can be written on the mandala. For instance, a child can write, "I love squelching in the mud," because it's something that makes him or her feel happy inside. Anything that makes you feel happy or joyful is all good energy.

This 'work' is my spiritual focus. I do believe God lives in my DNA, that God is part of my everything, and that I am part of everything. It's my place to polish myself in every moment; to be aware in every moment of what I think, what I say and what I do. Yes, some days there's bit of 'traffic;' then okay, time to breathe. There are special breathing techniques, but for me, it's a reminder to polish; take the rag and polish my soul.

I can remember my spiritual teacher saying one time, "Too many of you are too hard on yourselves. You see a tiny little spec of dirt on yourself and you think that you are failing at something." To use the analogy of a silver teapot, when silver is tarnished it goes black. If you don't polish silver teapots they go black; then you need to get the polish and clean them. You don't know unless you polish the teapot, that it's really brilliant silver underneath. Brilliant. That's who we are. But if we see a tiny little spec on the silver, we notice it. Whereas when it was tarnished black, we didn't notice the spec because it was all black. I often say to people that we are the polished silver teapot, and the little spec is just something that we can look at and say, "Hey. I'm doing a really great job, and I'm endeavouring to be happy." You know, whether I'm going to the supermarket to do the shopping, whether I'm cleaning the stove at home, there's no difference between that or going to a prayer meeting. For myself, I'm striving to be the very best I can be and the happiest I can be. When a room is all-dark, you can't see anything. But then, when you turn the light on, you can see everything. It's a bit like the teapot. It's what we open ourselves up to. For me, it's an ongoing polishing.

Another thing that's really important on our agenda at the moment is called the Fuji Declaration. It's something that anyone can sign, regardless of one's faith or spiritual tradition. In 2010, I wrote a book. It's never been edited and I wrote it just as it came to me; some parts flow more easily than others, and most of it is written from a spirit and intuitive perspective. I started writing it from a program called 'Na-No-Wri-Mo,' which is 'National Novel Writing Month in November.' It now has hundreds of thousands of people around the world who write in November. It wasn't until late in 2014 that I was willing to let anybody else ever read it. I thought, "Okay, it's time." It doesn't matter what I've written, and if people read it, that's absolutely fine. In 2008, my mother passed away from a stroke. That was another 'Jen shake-up' to find out about compassion and love. As I wrote my book, I found that quite a few deep feelings such as this came through.

This is my story. I find my spiritual journey is often a challenge. But it's beautiful. I love it, and I meet people like all of you. These are gifts that I cherish, and they continue to grow, and I'm very thankful.

Questions and comments from the audience

Q. Jenny. How long was your training?

The training itself wasn't so long. The home training could take whatever time you felt you needed. For myself, to complete 80-hours of meditation, the home training was from the end of March to the end of April. Then I went to Japan in August 1999 to complete the training. I work for the organisation now. I'm a staff member and the contact person in Australia and the Oceania countries. If people are interested in anything that we do, then I can travel to places where people want me to go to.

The Japanese organisation of Byakko Shinko Kai has members who are Buddhist and Shinto. Shinto believe in gratitude to nature and being connected to nature. Outside Japan, I've got friends who belong to the organisation who are Jewish, Muslim, Catholic and Anglican. They can do the internal 'work' with Byakko Shinko Kai and still follow their own traditional faith if they want to. I think I've stepped into something that for me is all encompassing. That's why I do a lot of interfaith work in Geelong, because for me, all faiths are aspects of the one and that's what I love. One of the things I really love is that there is oneness in diversity. Oneness doesn't mean blancmange or mixed up soup. Oneness is to have that diversity, honour it, cherish it and have people share it with one another and respect one another no matter what they believe. This is why I was drawn to the Byakko Shinko Kai, because for me, it encompassed what was already in me, even as a child.

Crunchy Tuna Surprise

Serves 4-6
Preparation time: 30min

INGREDIENTS

1 tbsp butter or margarine
1 tbsp plain flour
500ml skim milk
¼ cup firmly packed grated parmesan cheese or cheese of your choice
Tabasco sauce or mustard, to taste (optional)
½ cup firmly packed, grated, extra light tasty cheese
1 cup cooked rice
425g can tuna in spring water, flaked
8 cups salad, to serve

Crunchy topping:
1 tbsp butter, melted
1 cup cornflakes, crushed

METHOD

1. Preheat oven to 200°C. Lightly grease a deep casserole dish. Set aside.
2. Melt butter in saucepan over medium heat. Add flour and stir for 1 minute until smooth. Remove from heat. Gradually add milk, stirring constantly. Return to heat, stirring, until sauce comes to the boil. Reduce heat to low.
3. Add parmesan (or cheese of choice) and tabasco/mustard (I use mustard). Add tasty cheese, reserving a small amount. Stir until cheeses have melted.
4. In the prepared dish, arrange half the rice, tuna, and cheese sauce in a layer. Repeat, using the remaining half of the ingredients.
5. I usually mix all the ingredients gently, leaving chunks of tuna, rather than layering, but both work well.
6. Make the crunchy topping: melt butter in small saucepan. Mix in crushed cornflakes. Sprinkle topping over dish. Top with remaining cheese.
7. Bake: for 15 minutes or until heated through. Serve with a large salad.

Noriko Jede - White Butterfly

My name is Noriko Jede. I was born in a very rural area in Japan called Akita Province. When I was born, we had four generations living in the same home. The younger children were only two; me and my younger sister. It was a big house and a big property, so as children, we jumped around and rode our bicycles as we pleased. It was a very, very rural area and very beautiful countryside; we enjoyed nature. It was so beautiful. And everything was made by hand; vegetables, noodles… my grandmother made everything. At that time when I was small, there was no such thing as biscuits or cakes in Japan. We did not have it for morning tea or afternoon tea. What we had were many types of pickles that my grandmother made; they were so tasty. I wish I could learn a little bit more about this style of cooking so I could make it now. But it's a bit late now. I guess I can still vividly remember that beautiful place where I was born. I went to primary school there, and walked about half an hour to school. In junior high school, it was a 45-minute walk. Every morning and every evening my sister and I walked to school together. For three years during high school, I went to the city and had to take the train and the bus. After I finished high school, I went to Tokyo.

I had to leave my parent's house to go to the university in Tokyo. That is when my life totally changed. Because the lifestyle in Tokyo is so different to my rural village, my parents didn't allow me to stay in the dormitory, so I had to stay with my aunt. It was really, really hard in the beginning because she was so very strict. I just wanted to study, so there was no freedom when I would come back to my aunt's home after university. My aunt didn't like me studying. She said I have to learn how to cook and how to clean up, otherwise I can't get a man in the future. She was a typical

Herstory

Japanese woman. So she taught me all kinds of cooking, even some fundamental methods. That's how she taught me. She taught me how to eat, how to sit down at the table; she showed me. Before I went to Tokyo, actually when I was in year six, the last year of primary school, my grandfather passed away. Since that time, I started thinking about life – the meaning of life, especially when I first saw the funeral. In Japan, everyone is cremated – nobody is buried. Cremation shocked me and I was in such pain. Everybody was cremated; that was totally shocking for me, it was totally painful. Since that time, I searched for something, something other than Buddhism. That's what started my path towards Christianity.

I was born in such a rural area where there was no Bible or church, but when I went to high school, there was one Catholic Church. There, I went to Bible study and started going to church a little bit. That's my past, starting a different way than the Buddhism that my parents believed in. I searched for another way. My aunty used to be a Christian, but somehow, she was so disappointed with the priest, so she never allowed me to go to the church. But I just went to the Catholic Church, hiding there, hiding from her, because somehow I just liked it. Just being in the church, I received so much peace and calm. In Japan, going to university is hard work; it is hard studying because of strict examinations. Then, after going to university, you also have to work so much. Just dropping into the church was really, really my peaceful resting place, so I just kept going. When I went back home to my aunt, she didn't allow me to study, so I just studied somewhere outside the home. She just showed me how to cook. This continued, and finally I finished university, studying English, linguistics and English literature.

I graduated, and now the time came to get a job. But my auntie wanted me to get married rather than get a job. That was her only purpose. I didn't know any boys because my aunty was so strict about relationships with men. So she started bringing photos for the arranged marriage. I think it was popular at the time when I was young. So, many photos came. But somehow, it didn't work out anyway, and I just got a job. It was strict to get a job in Japan at that time. It was very difficult. But I got a job with an American trust company, Morgan Guaranty Trust Company of New York. I worked in the import and export department as an English translator. I worked in Tokyo and I enjoyed the job quite a bit. The people were from America, the President of the company was American, and another had a Scottish accent. Of course, there were a lot of Japanese people because it was a business in Japan. All the photos for an arranged marriage continued to come. My auntie tried to arrange a marriage. But it didn't work out, and now I am getting kind of old by Japanese standards.

I visited my parent's house taking a break from work. There was a big department store, so I did shopping. There was a group of people there doing something and some of them approached me with a pamphlet, but they didn't talk to me. On the other side of that department store was the Catholic Church that I first went to when I was in high school. I walked into the church and there was a Catholic father inside, but somehow he was a bit strange. He had an unusual attitude towards me. I don't know what happened. I talked to this father, but then he said, "What are they doing in front of that department store?" You know, I had no idea. But he asked me. He thought that I came from that group.

Actually, that group consisted of members from the Family Federation for World Peace and Unification (FFWPU). Anyway, the Catholic priest was very much against the Unification Church and that's the reason he didn't treat me well. I didn't feel comfortable so I left and walked in the direction of the railway station to go back home. Then, there was another group of people. They were also from the Unification Church and they were watching people passing by. Just before getting on the train, I was approached by a lady. She didn't know I was reading the Bible or that I went to the Catholic Church. Actually, I had a lot of questions about the Bible that I couldn't understand. So I asked her a lot of questions. She couldn't answer all the questions so she introduced me to a lecturer and he said, "Please come and listen to the seminars." They both invited me to the very humble and small house which was the local Unification Church. I went to the lecture; it was an absolutely beautiful lecture and I was so affected. At that time, the lectures were written down, no PowerPoint, just a blackboard and chalk. The introductory lecture was fantastic. I still remember it; I was so moved and I just had to keep going to finish the whole series of lectures.

Finally, I finished the series of lectures and I didn't know what to do. I finally decided to join this Church. I worked in the local church a little bit because I joined the local FFWPU Church and soon afterwards, I went to the headquarters in Tokyo where I worked for a quite a long time.

After some time, I was recommended to attend the Church Blessing of the FFWPU. The purpose of the Church Blessing is to create the beautiful families. The fundamental philosophy is so different to a girlfriend and boyfriend relationship. If enemy nations are matched together as a couple, this is the best way to create peace; the children love both cultures because they love both their parents. For instance, during World War II, Japan and America fought each other.

I was matched with an Australian man of German origin. Kurt came to Australia when he was six or seven years old. He was Australian, but his nature was largely German. He used to speak German with his parents. He passed away in 2001, so that was a very difficult time for my three children and I. We received the Blessing in America in 1982, and then we came back to Australia and our children were all born here. When my husband passed away, my children were in year 12, year 11 and the youngest was only ten years old. Now he is 25. So it was such a difficult time; the children were at a sensitive age. The youngest boy, he knows a little bit about his father, but there is a gap in the process of his growth; there was no father's love. So I had to take all the responsibility for raising my children; I had to look after the financial situation as well. I had to support the family and myself. The children were still school-aged so there were the education costs as well. It was such a difficult time, but now, they've grown up and settled down. I turned 67 the other day, on the 10th October. Reflecting back, I had to go through such a big wave, but I had to save myself, my life. Every time I overcame a big wave, I learnt something. I couldn't stop the wave, even with tears, I had to overcome it.

(left to right) Won, Joon, Kurt, Noriko and Jalia - taken just before Kurt passed away

After Kurt's passing, I would hear noises outside. "What's this noise? It's dark already. What's this noise?" This happened so many times. Maybe the children pushed the doorbell, but nobody was there. This was a sign for me. My husband would come to me wearing a very humble jacket that he used to wear when we were first married. If something serious happened to us, he would come to me. When he appeared to me, he was surrounded in total darkness, but his spirit was a bright light. The spot around him was black, so I couldn't tell where he was in the spirit world; I couldn't tell. One day, my youngest son had a dream where he looked into the spirit world with a telescope trying to find out where his father was. But he couldn't find his father. Then I thought I had to let my husband go, because I hadn't let him go yet. My husband was such a quiet person, but when my children and I sat down in the lounge, I felt he was standing beside me. Most of the time, I was so tired, but he kept coming. I could feel some cool air coming when he came beside me. But not now; after ten years, he's different and I feel he's more free. He's like a butterfly, a white butterfly. So now I think he is more free in the spirit world.

Q. When you see the white butterfly, how do you know it is your husband?

Rev. Moon told a story about a young missionary who was sent to Czechoslovakia during the communist era. She was persecuted and killed because of her faith. When this happened, Rev. Moon said that she came to him as a butterfly. When Rev. Moon saw the butterfly, he knew that she was free; her spirit was free because a butterfly can fly anywhere. Since I read this story, whenever the butterfly comes, I feel it is my husband, Kurt. The butterflies come in sunny places around my roses, and I feel it.

My life is very different now, but it was difficult at the beginning; very, very difficult. Not only on the individual level, but at the family level as well. All I could do was just to go forward. Now I'm grateful I could grow internally. Some people question this blessing and the difficulties. But finally I learnt, this was Heavenly God's love. If I didn't go through that big wave or rough road, I probably couldn't have grown and become like my present self. Now every time I go through a rough road or when a big wave comes, I know that I will learn many things. Now, if the big wave comes, I think I know how to cope and how to go through it. Now, I am just so grateful because of everything I came to know – Rev. Moon and the Unification Church. Now I understand; everything was love, just love. So I am so grateful.

This is my story.

Sushi - A traditional Japanese dish

Serves 4-6

INGREDIENTS

2 cup short-grain rice
1 tbsp sugar
5 tbsp rice vinegar
100g fresh fish fillet (such as salmon, tuna, ocean trout)
1 small lebanese cucumber
½ avocado
4 nori sheets
Wasabi to taste
Pickled ginger (to serve)
Japanese soy sauce (to serve)

METHOD

1. Rinse rice under cold water and drain well. Place rice and 2cups of water in a saucepan and bring to boil. Decrease heat to low and simmer uncovered for 12-15 minutes, stirring occasionally, until the water is absorbed. Remove from heat and let stand with lid on for a further 10 minutes.
2. Place rice in a large bowl. In a separate bowl, combine the sugar, 2 tablespoons vinegar and 1 teaspoon salt, and pour over rice. Stir to combine. Cover a flat tray with aluminum foil and spread rice on it to cool. The rice should be completely cool before using.
3. Choose from a variety of fillings. We use normally fresh salmon and tuna, cucumber and avocado. Prepare the fish and vegetables by slicing into batons abut 5cm long. Set aside. Meanwhile, combine remaining vinegar and 300ml cold water in a bowl.
4. Place 1 nori sheet, shiny-side down, on a bamboo mat. Make sure the longest edge of nori is at the top of the mat. Dip hands in water mixture and spread a quarter of rice over bottom two-thirds of nori, leaving a small border around edge.
5. Spread a thin line of wasabi along the middle of the rice and arrange a little of the fish and vegetables alongside the wasabi. Gently lift the end of the mat closest to you and roll it over the ingredients to enclose.
6. Continue rolling the mat forward to make a complete roll. With one hand on top, gently roll mat back and forth a few times to make a nice round shape. Use a sharp knife to slice the rolls at 2cm intervals. Serve with pickled ginger, soy sauce and extra wasabi.

Layer the ingredients on the seaweed and the bed of rice

Roll the sushi using the bamboo sushi roll

Slice the sushi roll using a wet knife

Tempura - A traditional Japanese dish

INGREDIENTS

¾ cup plain flour
¼ cup corn flour
Pinch of bicarbonate of soda
1 egg, lightly whisked
1 cup soda water, chilled
Vegetable oil, to deep-fry
Plain flour, extra, to coat
1 carrot, peeled, diagonally sliced
¼ butternut pumpkin, peeled, seeded, thinly sliced
1 red capsicum, quartered, seeded
1 small eggplant, thinly sliced
1 bunch asparagus, trimmed
300g green king prawns, peeled, deveined, leaving tails intact
Light soy sauce (to serve)
Wasabi (to serve)

Serves 4-6

Tempura batter

Deep frying the Tempura pieces until light brown

METHOD

1. Sift the flour, cornflour and bicarbonate of soda in a medium bowl. Make a well in the centre. Add the egg and soda water and use chopsticks to gently whisk until just combined. Place the bowl in a larger bowl filled with iced water.
2. Add enough oil to a large saucepan to reach a depth of 6cm. Place over high heat. To test when oil is ready, a cube of bread turns golden-brown in 10 seconds.
3. Place extra flour on a plate. Dip the vegetables in the flour to lightly coat. Dip one quarter of the vegetables, one at a time, into the batter. Shake off any excess. Deep-fry for 2-3 minutes or until golden brown and tender.
4. Use a slotted spoon to transfer to a plate lined with paper towel. Repeat with remaining vegetables. Dip prawns in the extra flour to lightly coat. Dip prawns in the batter, one at a time, then deep-fry for 3-4 minutes or until golden brown and cooked through.
5. Place vegetables and prawns on a serving platter. Serve immediately with soy sauce and wasabi

Patricia Beke Mayele - From Congo to Australia

Good evening. My name is Colette Patricia Beke. I'm from the Democratic Republic of Congo. I was born the youngest in a family of six children, one boy and five girls. Three months after my Mum got pregnant with me, she got divorced and had to manage by herself. When I reached six years of age, my brother and sisters shared their part in raising me. One sibling took me for a couple of years, and then another took me. I had four elder sisters; they were all married, but, after about ten years, they got divorced too, and this made me very sad. I was thinking about my life and decided that I would not get married; I would become a religious sister instead. I went to boarding school, and I started going to church meetings and learning about how to become a nun. But the head nun told me that they were not taking young girls into the church because after they finished school, they would get married and wouldn't follow the path.

After high school, I left my hometown and came to the capital city because I had nowhere to live. My Mum was an orphan too. My mother married when she was young, but she was alone because she didn't have any brothers or sisters. In my culture, we are matriarchal; children are taken care of by the mother's family. As my Mum had no family, I had nowhere to go. She had to talk with a family friend, and they took me to my cousin. He had joined the Family Federation for World Peace and Unification (FFWPU) and he testified to me about church. Upon learning about the Divine Principle of the FFWPU, I changed my mind and decided, "Okay I can get married; it is a good way." Then I started looking for true love. I don't know why, but unfortunately, I didn't find my true love. I could not find a good partner even though I went to the Matching Ceremony four times.

In 1996, the Rwandans, who are our neighbouring nation, invaded Congo and attacked the capital city. My family fled from the city, and I followed a group of friends, ending up in Benin as a refugee. I stayed in Benin for 12 years, and there I found a good partner and we went to the Blessing Wedding Ceremony. Unfortunately, after our Blessing, he 'flew' away, and said that he didn't have any money and couldn't take care of someone. I followed him so that I could convince him that we could make something together, and so we stayed together. I was still a refugee and applied through immigration, to be accepted as an international refugee. That decision to leave Benin with two children was very difficult. My husband and I fought on the issue of how to settle our family. It was not easy, but in the end, I was accepted to come to Australia. However, my husband was not a refugee, and he could not come with me to Australia, so he stayed in Benin.

I spoke French and had to learn English in Australia; it was very hard, really hard. I started with Level I English. My vision was to be a nurse; I studied nursing in Benin and just when I finished my degree, it was time to leave for Australia. Upon learning English, I started with a Certificate III in Educare. I did one and a half years of study. In my last placement, my clinical educator said that she didn't see me wash my hands and did not feel happy to give me a pass. I was really disappointed; I cried a lot. The school asked me to repeat the last subject, but I refused and I started another course in Disability Certificate IV. But I really liked nursing, so I went to enrol again. This month, I will start again and re-do the last subject in nursing and try again. Now I'm just looking for a job, but I cannot find a job. It's very difficult, but I think it's just a challenge; I'm not going to give up and I am trying to go ahead.

Questions and comments from the audience

Q. What is your husband's situation now?

When I first arrived, I was living in Geelong. A lady from the Diversitat Settlement Services told me she could help me with my husband's situation and fill out the immigration forms. I told her that my husband was not a refugee. However, she gave me the refugee form, and because of my poor English, I didn't understand that it was the wrong form. I sent this incorrect form to my husband, but because he does not speak English either, he signed the form also. The Department of Immigration refused his entry to Australia because he signed the form to immigrate to Australia as a refugee. Now I'm waiting for my citizenship. I've already passed the test, and I am waiting for the ceremony. If I receive the citizenship, then maybe it will be easy for my husband to immigrate. I'm collecting every document the Department of Immigration needs.

Q. Tell us about your children. How old are they?

I have two boys; the eldest one is going on fourteen, and the younger one is going on twelve. We try to manage. They are okay.

Comment: Language is always a barrier isn't it? If you had the right form and the right advice about how to proceed, you would not be alone for so long, and your children would have their father. It is heart-breaking when you do not know where to go for help.

Patricia: In Geelong, it was really lonely because the authorities put all the Congolese together in the one place. But Congo is such a big country, with four main languages. The Congolese who came at the same time as me were from Eastern Congo. They cannot speak French or Lingala; they speak Swahili, and I cannot speak Swahili. I felt terribly isolated; the communication was very difficult, and I was feeling really lonely. If I wanted to find food at the food store, I locked the children at home. The authorities told me that if the police saw this, they would take my children. So I decided to move closer to Melbourne and moved to Hoppers Crossing. However, the caseworker in Hoppers Crossing didn't understand me; they didn't connect me with anyone who could assist me. I came, and I was by myself; everything was very hard, very heart-breaking.

Q. So what kept you going? What gave you strength and spirit?

Personally, my life has never been happy; I never find life easy. I decided not to have children, because maybe my children will end up having the same life as me. But, when I followed the 'Principles,' in the Divine principle of the FFWPU, I decided, "Yes. It's a good way. Maybe I can have children." By the time I had my two children, I found that life was not easy at all. However, I try to persevere because even if I suffer, my kids will not suffer like I have. I will do the best I can; as long I can live, I will go. If I cannot get an easier life now, never mind, my kids can get it and I will fight for them to have a good life.

Q. Do you communicate with your husband?

Yes. We communicate via telephone because he doesn't have the basic computer skills to use email. If I cannot call him, he cannot call me again. If I have money, I call him and we talk.

Comment: I think continuing with your nursing will give you a better chance in life. I came to Australia in 1982 as a midwife. When I registered to do Nursing

Counselling, I was told that my qualifications did not apply in Australia. Therefore, I enrolled in nursing instead of midwifery. In the following year, I went to university. There are ways you can break through, so just keep trying.

Comment: When I hear your story I see the power of love; the maternal heart to give something to your children to make life better, whatever it takes. I think this is an incredible strength we have as women.

Patricia: Thank you. This is my story.

Ceebu Jen (Rice and Smoked Fish)

Here is an account of smoked fish by Harry Hamilton Johnston a British explorer who visited the Congo river region just at the start of the European scramble to colonize Africa following the Berlin Conference of 1884. He writes, "One tribe on the Upper Congo makes quite a traffic in smoked fish, which they sell to the resident tribes. It is a most common sight to see a group of these Ba-yansi people established temporarily on a great sandbank in the middle of the river, smoking the newly-caught fish over immense wood fires." Johnston goes on to say, "I have often bought and eaten these smoked fish. . . they are delicious—yes, emphatically delicious."

Below is smoked fish recipe from the same region.

Ceebu Jen (Rice and Smoked Fish)

INGREDIENTS

Sauce and vegetables:
1 cup red palm oil (substitute a vegetable oil)
2 chopped onions
Medium sized piece of dried smoked fish (such as cod or herring).
3 pounds of whole cleaned sea bass, haddock, or halibut fish steak
1 can of tomato paste
4 whole tomatoes
1 or more chopped carrots, cassava, potatoes or yams
1 hot chilli pepper
Small portion of vegetables (such as chopped cabbage, squash, eggplant, zucchini).

Stuffing mixture:
2 chopped green, yellow, or red sweet peppers
1 chopped scallion or onion
1 minced garlic
1/3 cup of fresh parsley, bay leaf, or cilantro
Salt to taste
Hot chilli peppers to taste

METHOD

1. Prepare the stuffing mixture by combining the stuffing mixture ingredients and grinding them into a paste, adding a little oil or water if needed. Many cooks include what seems to be an essential in Africa: a Maggi cube.
2. Cut deep slits into the fish (but not all the way through) and stuff them with the roof mixture. Heat the oil in a large pot.
3. Fry the onions and smoked fish for a few minutes and then remove the fish and set aside. Stir the tomato paste and a cup of water into the oil in the pot. Add the root vegetables and tubers and the hot chilli pepper.
4. Add water to partially cover them. Bring to a boil, reduce heat and simmer for 30 minutes or more. Add the leaf and fruit vegetables, place the fried fish on top of them, and continue to simmer for an additional twenty minutes or until the vegetables are tender. The fish and all the vegetables and set them aside, keeping them warm.
5. Remove a cup or two of the vegetable broth and set it aside. Add the rice to the vegetable broth. Add water or remove liquid as necessary to obtain two parts liquid to one part rice. Bring to a boil, cover, and simmer on very low heat until the rice is cooked about twenty minutes. It should stick a little to the bottom of the pot.
6. Find the hot chili among the vegetables. Combine it to the reserved vegetable broth in a small saucepan and bring to a slow boil. Remove and discard the pepper and put the sauce into a dish or gravy boat.
7. When the rice is done turn the pot over onto a large serving platter. Arrange the fish and vegetables around the serving plate. Garnish as desired. Serve with Cassava and Fufu Cassava (see accompanying recipes) or with rice.

Fufu (Congolese style)

Fufu (Foo-foo, Foufou, Foutou, Fu fu) is to Western and Central Africa cooking what mashed potatoes are to traditional European-American cooking. Fufu is a starchy accompaniment for stews or other dishes with sauce. For several centuries, Fufu has been in the Congolese culture.

The Fufu is a dish that is very important to Congolese because it is a staple food. This dish is composed of water and corn flour, sometimes mixed with cassava flour. It contains iron, calcium, and vitamin A, as it is a very substantial meal. Fufu is not only eaten in the Democratic Republic of Congo, but it is eaten in other countries in Africa. However, in some African countries, the Fufu is made with water mixed with plantain, cocoyam, maize, rice, instant potatoes flakes, or yams. Furthermore, the Congolese eat Fufu at least once a day. It is usually eaten at noon and if they have to eat it a second time during the day, it would be for supper. They eat it with vegetables, meat, fish or pepper. For example, my mom would cook it with chicken and cooked cassava leaves mixed with other vegetables such as cucumbers, zucchini and several other vegetables.

INGREDIENTS

500ml water
100g of corn flour

METHOD

1. Pour the water into the pan and bring to a boil.
2. Add the corn flour.
3. Simmer for a few seconds and then stir. When the dough begins to be thick, add the remaining flour and mix until it is thick, but soft. Now the Fufu is ready to be served.

Fufu made with Yams

INGREDIENTS

2kg yams or equal parts yams and plantain bananas (use large, white or yellow yams, no sweet potatoes)
1 tsp butter (optional)

METHOD

1. Place yams in large pot and cover with cold water. Bring to a boil and cook until the yams are soft (approximately 30min).
2. Remove the pot from heat and cool yams with running water. Drain.
3. Remove the peels from yams. Add butter.
4. Put the yams in a bowl (or back in the empty pot) and mash with a potato masher, then beat and stir with a wooden spoon until completely smooth. This might take two people: one to hold the bowl and the other to stir.
5. Shape the Fufu into balls and serve immediately with meat stew or any dish with a sauce or gravy.

Pondu (Cassava Leave)

Pondu is a traditional Congolese recipe for a classic stew of cassava leaves (Saka-saka) flavoured with onion, red palm oil, chillies, garden eggs and tinned sardines or mackerel.

Note: You can find frozen cassava leaves at some Asian food stores. You can substitute cassava leaves with collard greens, kale, cabbage, turnip greens, spinach, or a mix of these.

INGREDIENTS

4 cups minced cassava leaves
½ cup minced celery
1 ½ large red or white onion
2 large or 3 small eggplants (Thai green eggplant or possibly purple eggplant)**, diced**
2 tbsp oil
1 large clove garlic
1 green capsicum
¼ tsp salt
1 can of sardines or any kind of canned fish
Fresh chillies pounded to a paste (optional)

METHOD

1. Heat 2 tablespoons of oil in a pan over medium heat.
2. Add the onions, celery, eggplant, capsicum and garlic and fry for about 5 minutes, or until soft.
3. Wash and finely shred the cassava leaves then add to the pan.
4. Drain the sardines and cut into small pieces then stir into the cassava leaf mix.
5. Season to taste with salt and or chilli paste.
6. Cover and reduce to a low simmer then cook for 30 minutes or until the cassava leaves are tender.

Serve with Fufu (see accompanying recipe), rice or couscous.

Concetta Surtees - Life of Gratitude

My name is Concetta Surtees. I was born in 1963 in the small town of Sinagra, Sicily. I descend from loving parents, Tindo and Rosina, and we lived on a farm together.

Life was very simple; we had organic food and spring water, and we supported ourselves financially by growing and picking hazelnuts. In 1971, when I was eight years old, my parents decided to migrate to Perth, Australia, where Mum and Dad's siblings had already migrated. At that time, Egypt and Israel were in conflict, therefore, we could not travel via the Suez Canal and had to sail around Africa. We boarded the ship, Galileo Galilei, and 26 days later, we arrived in Perth. My extended family, cousins, aunties and uncles welcomed us very affectionately.

I went to an English school even though I could not speak English. I developed a circle of friends, and got accustomed to the lifestyle. But after 12 months, my Mum and Dad decided that life was much better for us in Sicily where the rest of the family was. So after one and a half years, we came back to Sinagra. Life was really very different because we lived in a little house on the side of the mountain with no electricity or road. My Dad brought electricity to the house and made a road so that our house could be a little more modernised. Life was very quiet, with few visitors or friends coming home compared to life in Perth. I felt quite lonely and missed my friends and cousins in Perth. I attended primary and middle school in my little town, and when I was 15 years old, I attended an accounting high school in Capo d'Orlando, which is a city on the north-east coast of Sicily. I took the bus every morning and every afternoon. It was a public school; there were no Catholic schools in Italy unless you were an orphan. When I was 20, I graduated from accounting school and specialised in tax income. All my teenage years in Sinagra were spent dreaming about moving away because I was the only child until my parents gave birth to my sister when I was 15 years old. I didn't have much opportunity to spend time with friends because our home was so isolated.

When I was 21 years old, I moved away from Sinagra to Milan to find employment as a tax accountant. Life seemed quite good, but inside my heart, there was always some emptiness; I always asked myself, "Is there something more to life?" One day when I was window-shopping in one of the busy streets of Milan, I met a beautiful girl named Potensia; we are still friends 30 years later. She passed me a pamphlet about the hope and issues of young people, and how young people could make a difference and find a better way of living. Afterwards, I was invited to a weekend workshop located on the side of a mountain. It was a religious mountain with the 12 steps of Jesus, Via Crucis (Stations of the Cross). In Italy there are many monuments of the Stations of the Cross. At the end of Via Crucis, there was a beautiful hotel where the workshop was held; the outline of the syllabus was taught and has become part of my life for the last 30 years. The teachings of the Divine Principle are very simple – find God and be able to create a spiritual relationship with God. Keep your purity, and prepare yourself for marriage with somebody who is also preparing themselves; then create a family with a loving mother and father who can give birth to beautiful, blessed children who are able to make a difference in this world due to the love and the education they received through their family.

Through the teachings of the Family Federation for World Peace and Unification (FFWPU), I was able to connect with God more, and prepare myself to create a family that God would be proud of. For the next three years, I worked as a missionary by helping people in the community; I helped them physically, spiritually and emotionally. In 1989, I had the privilege of being invited to an international matching wedding ceremony. Yes, John, my Australian husband and I, were a match made in heaven right before it became fashionable, and we're so proud of that. Through the Family Federation guided by Rev. Dr. Sun Myung Moon, we're promoting families with parents who originate from different cultural, religious, national or racial backgrounds; for them to be loving parents, educating their children to break some of the ethnic barriers that have typically resulted in conflict throughout history.

During the cold winter of January 1989, I went to Seoul, Korea for the matching and blessing. I was in a room with more than a thousand people, and my beloved husband was there as well. We had the privilege to be matched by Rev. Dr. Sun Myung Moon, with the option to accept the match or not; we decided to accept. Three days later, we took our Blessing vows and promised to never break our union to be together; not just here on earth, but also in the spirit world. Our matching and Blessing Ceremony was unique, because after the Blessing we had an engagement period of about three years, after which we started our family together. This three-year period gave us time to understand and get to know one another and we were able to start our family union with a much better chance of success. People think that having a good marriage starts with love at first sight, but it does not matter how you meet. As a couple, you need to work really very hard at the relationship, and you need to have a common goal. That's what John and I have; we had a common goal; we wanted to have a family that God could be proud of and one that the world would admire. This has been our work for the last 27 years.

John and I stayed in Korea for about five years working as missionaries teaching English and helping the community. It was a very important cultural education for us because we could experience how people live a different way of life. In 1984, we decided to move to Australia because we wanted to raise our family next to their grandparents, John's parents. We wanted our children to have the experience of their grandparent's love, and to set up the infrastructure to create a functional and loving extended family. In 1985, we were privileged to welcome our first-born son, Alistair. We chose Alistair Luke because Alistair is a derivative of Alisandra, meaning 'conductor of human kind.' Luke means 'light,' therefore, his full name means 'light and conductor of human kind.' Twenty years later when we look at Alistair, we find that he's able to connect with people deeply, and all his peers are able to find inspiration and advice from him. Therefore, I do believe that a person's name has such a profound meaning when it's used. At the time when we chose Alistair's name, we really didn't know the impact.

In 1996, our second-born, Alicia, was born. She was premature, but she never gives up. Her name is Alicia Tayana, which means 'girl from noble birth.' Alicia never compromises and always chooses what's best for everybody; she is a fighter. In 1999, we were blessed with our last beautiful girl. Her name is Odette Leticia. Odette means 'home-maker,' and Leticia means 'grace;' she really is a home-maker. Whenever you talk to Odette, you'll feel comfortable. You will never feel she is disagreeing with you or means you harm; she is always loving and welcoming. When we look back on how difficult it was to choose our children's name, I'm proud to say that we chose good names for our children. When Alicia was born, she was a caesarean birth. The operation was scheduled for 3.00pm, and at 2.50pm, John and I were still in a coffee shop discussing what name we should choose for our coming baby girl. Alistair was nameless for one week. My parents-in-law were unhappy because everybody was asking about the name, and we had a child who was nameless. I just want to make a point that names and the words we call people, and how we deal with people, have a certain power.

For me, coming to Australia was not very easy. I had to learn the Australian way, which is emotionally very different from the Italian way. In Italy, you don't need an invitation to visit someone's home and have a coffee together. Here, I have to make an appointment, even to have a cup of coffee with my mother-in-law. It's been really quite difficult to get used to; but after a while, you do. My English language was basic; I had to fit in with my children's playgroup, kindergarten and the parents of my children's school friends, and make sure that I was one of them. Sometimes, it was really very hard to follow the conversation due to having a different cultural background. I've been so fortunate that I've been able to create very good friends. Even now, after so many years, we're still having dinners and coffees together; we're still looking after one another's children, and we admire how well our families and our children have been doing.

When raising a family to be functional and happy, there are different types of obstacles that come. When raising a family in a different country, you don't have the support of your own family. When the first child comes, there's distraction. When the second child comes, there's more distraction, and when the third one comes, there's even more distraction… There are financial, working and housing problems, and of course, there are affection problems that have to be worked through in a marriage. But, if you really want a good marriage, and if you really have a goal together as husband and wife, if you really promise to be faithful with complete dedication, there is no reason why couples shouldn't be able to create loving and functional families, and create an environment where children can grow strong with values, and stand up for what's important; for example, standing up for human rights and making a difference in this world.

One day my daughter, Alicia, and I, were talking about how many of her school friends have parents who are divorced and how difficult it is for her friends. I asked Alicia, "Why do you think our family works?" She said to me, "Well Mum, having dinner together helps." I thought, "Wow, it's that simple?" But maybe it is just that simple; having quality time together as a family, and being there for your husband, your wife, your children and keep on going.

In conclusion, John and I have been really, really blessed to have found one another. We do believe we are soulmates, and we have so much gratitude to have been given three healthy children – children who have the strength to go out there and make a difference. Thank you.

Concetta shared her story while very weak and knowing her time was near. She passed in Autumn of 2016, surrounded by her husband and three children. Concetta's parents flew from Sicily to share the last two months with her.

Chilli Cream Pasta - A delicious family recipe

Serves 4-6

INGREDIENTS

1 long red chilli (mild chilli)
2 cloves garlic
3 rashes lean bacon
½ red Spanish onion
Hand full of button mushrooms
Tin of whole peeled tomatoes
(4 tomatoes)
300ml cooking cream
2 tbsp olive oil
Rock salt as per taste
500g short pasta

METHOD

1. Using a thick based frypan, place the olive oil in the pan.
2. Finely slice the garlic, bacon and onion. Place these in the oil with the whole chilli and brown over medium heat.
3. Add the sliced mushrooms and continue stirring so the mixture does not stick to the frypan.
4. Drain the can of tomatoes and add 4 tomatoes (without the liquid). Squash each tomato with a fork.
5. Add salt to taste and when sizzling take off the heat.
6. Cook the short pasta in boiling water as per pasta instructions. Drain the pasta and put aside. Do not wash the pasta with water (Italian style).
7. Place the frypan mixture back onto medium heat and add the cooking cream. When the mixture is bubbling, add the pasta and mix in.
8. If a hotter taste is required, crack open the whole chilli and mix into the pasta mixture. Otherwise, leave the chilli whole.

Catriona Devlin - Serving as a Brigidine Sister

My story goes back quite a way back to an island off the west coast of Scotland called the Isle of Tiree. I was born during the war when my father was overseas serving in the British Armed Forces. My mother was a foster child of a family on Tiree; she was surrounded by a lot of love, but in some ways she was very alone.

The Isle of Tiree is the most westerly of the Inner Hebrides. My father, John Devlin, came from Paisley near Glasgow, on the Scottish mainland. His family had lived there for a few generations and he grew up to become a builder/carpenter. At the start of the war he was stationed on the Island to help build an aerodrome, as many of the war planes refuelled there. So that was how he met my mother, Elizabeth Barr, who was looking after her foster mother there. Dad was then called up to serve in the Army and the two of them married in 1943. Soon after, Dad was stationed overseas in places like Yugoslavia, Greece, Italy and Israel. Mum often never knew where he was stationed as all the mail had to come through the Home Office in London. Actually, Dad was in Yugoslavia when I was born, and Mum sent a cable through to the Home Office to tell him he had a daughter.

Dad was Catholic and Mum had been brought up Protestant. While Dad was away, and while she was expecting me, Mum sometimes stayed with Dad's people on the mainland in Paisley. Upon marriage, she signed a document guaranteeing that she would bring up her children as Catholic, and so she decided to become a Catholic. She was quite a religious person already, and had attended a convent in Paisley to take instruction. When my father came back from the war, he found that she was now a Catholic. He hadn't done anything about it personally, because he didn't want to convince her one way or the other. Soon after Dad's return from the war, another daughter, Mairi, was born.

By then, Dad was re-entering civilian life and looking for work. There were few building opportunities available on the Island, so he was anxious to move his little family back to the mainland where his mother and some of his sisters still lived. Eventually we moved back to Paisley where two more children were born, Christine and Iain. By the time Christine was born, I think Britain was in a very bad way and Dad was anxious to get on. A lot of British people were migrating to Kenya at the time, so the decision was made that we would migrate there. However, Mum became pregnant with Iain, so these plans changed. The opportunity for migration to Australia then came up, and when Iain was only four months old, we migrated to Australia.

My parents then had three young children and Mum was still breastfeeding a fourth. We boarded a ship in early November 1950, arriving in Melbourne in mid-December. My father took work as a carpenter in the Latrobe Valley. The State Electricity Commission (SEC) had a house in Morwell ready for us, with food and furniture – a very different experience from that of the refugees and migrants from Europe who went to camps and didn't have this support. We were very fortunate.

After a few years, there was a period when there wasn't enough work in the Latrobe Valley so Dad tried to find work in Sydney, Tasmania and Cooma (NSW). This worried him as they had a young family and he was away from home a great deal. My mother's diaries give evidence of her own loneliness at this time too. Eventually this changed and life became easier and Dad built a house in Morwell. We all attended the local Sacred Heart Primary School run by the Josephite Sisters.

There was a time when Dad stopped going to Mass with us. I think it was related to the Labour Party split in 1955. Some members accused others of being too tied to Communism. It was a huge split and it caused a lot of trouble in Victoria in particular; it wasn't so evident in New South Wales. During these times, the priests were often taking sides and condemning some Labour Party figures from the pulpit. Dad found this involvement of the church in politics so offensive that he stopped going to church. This was a big shame for our family because now we had a father who didn't go to church any more. However, he always encouraged us to go.

It wasn't until 1963 when my father received the verdict of cancer that he resumed his church-going. From then on, my father never looked back and we never really asked him why there was a period when he stopped going to church. This was also the year I entered the convent. I suppose I'm sharing this because we weren't a particularly pious family but we were a church-going family. Times were different then. I think that both of my parents were really quite religious.

In 1958 the Brigidine Sisters were invited by the local bishop to work in the diocese of Sale, so they opened a secondary school for girls in Traralgon called Kildare College. That was the time when I was due to go into Year 9 I had won a prestigious junior government scholarship that would have covered the fees and books for any secondary school. However, Kildare was new and not yet registered. Dad was so proud of me and wanted me to use the scholarship so I was sent to Morwell High School – for two days! I was upset because all my friends were going to Kildare College. I must have brought terrible stories home from the high school about what the girls were talking about. Mum was so horrified that she went with me by bus to Traralgon to see the Head Sister, who eventually agreed to waive the fees. During this time at school in Traralgon, I remember an old friend of my mothers who said, "Be careful, if they take her for no fees, they might want her to be a nun." None of us took any notice, but I laugh about it when I think of it now, because I did join the nunnery I suppose – but not because of the fees being waived!

Kildare was a smallish school because it was just beginning. But I went through to Year 12 and matriculated, which was a big achievement in those days. In the senior years of school, we had annual three-day retreats during which time we had time to pray and think about life. A visiting priest would come to speak to us. There was always the discussion about, "What are you going to do with your life?" At times it seemed attractive to do what the nuns were doing. I wouldn't say I was very pious, but most mornings I would get on my bike and go to weekday Mass before going to school. That's very unusual now; we don't even have a Mass every morning. In those days, the two professions open to girls were nursing or and teaching. I knew I wanted to be a teacher; nursing never really appealed to me. Some girls left school a bit earlier and went into the bank. That was always considered a good job too. Options were very limited for girls.

There were times when I tried to say to my parents that I wanted to become a nun. But they wouldn't hear of it, particularly my father. I was too young and I was the oldest, so he wanted me to have a career. In primary school with the Josephite Sisters, the girls were encouraged to think about going to the Josephite Juniorate after Year 8, and finishing their education there, with a view to becoming a Novice and then a Josephite Sister. A few local girls had done this. My parents discouraged such a move. Dad said I was just interested in the dress ups, to look like a nun.

After matriculating I went to the Brigidine Teachers' Training Teachers' College in Malvern. At that time, several Orders had set up teachers' colleges and there was one in Malvern on High Street. There would have been about 50 young women from all over Victoria who started at the same time. In those days, Catholic teaching was a year in teacher's college and a year under supervision in a school. At the end of my year in teachers' college, I finally convinced my parents that I was serious about becoming a nun so I enrolled. So my year under supervision was also to be my first year in the Novitiate – a three-year period of training before you take your first vows. Then there is another five-year period in order to take your final vows.

Catriona (on the left) learning to be a Brigidine in 1963

While I was a first year Novice, I taught at Kildara College. I shared the Year 7 classes as a primary teacher with another Sister who was further on in the novitiate. I can still distinctly remember many of these students and their names! The year level had a reunion a few years ago which we both attended. It was lovely to meet them all again as grown women with families.

After three years in training as a novice I took my first vows. By this time, I was a qualified primary teacher and was appointed to the Convent at Mentone, where the Brigidine Sisters had a Secondary School, Kilbreda College. There were also many outlying Parish primary schools that we staffed. We lived on the premises of Kilbreda and looked after the boarders. We were allocated duties with boarders and also went out to teach at the outlying schools. I was to teach at St Patrick's Parish School in Mentone. In my first year I taught Prep, then Grade 5 in the next year. Then I received a letter from our then leader, asking me to go to Echuca to replace another Sister who was coming to Melbourne to complete her university studies. This meant I had to teach Year 12 French and

Australian History as well as a few other subjects. Someone who was on the Leadership team knew that I loved French and that I was quite good at French, so with a lot of effort and help, all went well and students did well in spite of me! The worst subject for me was Year 9 Science. I think I nearly blew the place up, even though I was following the experiment in the book! Although I didn't yet have a university degree, teaching at this level was considered good preparation for future university studies. You had little say then, in where you were posted; you just did what you were told and nobody really discussed it with you if all was going well. I loved those two years in Echuca even though I was always terrified that the students would find out that I didn't know much more than they did. I suppose that's true of most teachers at some stage. I met some of my previous students later on when I studied at Monash University; one was further ahead in her studies, but it didn't really matter as she had done well.

With students at Kibreda College in the 1980's

From Echuca I came back to Melbourne to make preparations to take my final vows and commit in a more final way to becoming a professed Brigidine Sister. I returned to Mentone again, but this time I was teaching at Kilbreda College and taught various levels there for about seven or eight years. After this, I was asked to return to Traralgon to be school principal at my old school, Kildare College. It was a really good experience and I was there for another seven years. Afterwards, I became principal at St Brigid's College in Horsham for four years, then took up a position as a secondary consultant for Religious Education at the Catholic Education Office in the Diocese of Sandhurst (Bendigo).

In 1994, the Leadership team offered me the opportunity to return to Ireland and Scotland to do some further study and look for work there. This was a wonderful opportunity to reconnect with relatives; I had come out to Australia as a child of six, so it was a long time since I had been back to Scotland. I still had some memories, and my family certainly kept in contact with our relatives, so it was great to catch up with them during that time. During this period, I completed some theological studies in Ireland and taught for a time in England. Upon my return, I resumed full-time teaching at Kilbreda; it seems that Kilbreda has been central to a lot of my teaching ministry; still today, it's quite close to my heart, both the staff and the students.

After ten years of teaching back at Kilbreda and being in charge of Religious Education in the school, I was offered the role of coming to Kildara Centre to work with adults in the area of adult faith development. It was a focus in spirituality that I had wanted to do for some time. The Sister who envisioned and began Kildara Centre and the Brigid's Well program there, was by then, terminally ill, so I took over her role in mid-2005; since then I have been working to develop these and further programs. At the moment, we're reviewing our focus and looking to future needs. I have found my role as Coordinator here, to be very life-giving.

Kildara Centre was formerly a girls' school, which opened in 1917. Unfortunately, it closed in the nineties. We weren't drawing girls from the local area; they were coming from outside the zone. This area is already serviced by a lot of girls' schools, so the decision was eventually made to close Kildara. The Brigidine Sisters kept what is now the Kildara Centre building, but the remainder of the school and convent land became residential apartment blocks. Two purpose-built houses were built on High Street and are reserved for our older sisters and a Victorian style house was kept for our leader's residence.

Questions and comments from the audience

Q. Tell us all about when you took your vows? Was there a calling?

I don't talk about a calling, but I felt an inner drive to serve God and to help make the world a better place. I felt strongly, that I could do that through education and teaching; they go hand-in-hand for me. The nuns who taught me during my school years inspired me by their lives. There probably was a calling, but it wasn't a call where I was knocked off my horse. This inspiration still drives me. The question isn't why I joined the nunnery; the real question is why I am still here! The answer is that I still experience that inner drive; I feel as though being a nun is who I'm meant to be, serving God and serving people, and doing all I can to make the world a better place.

Q. Tell us about the process of taking your vows.

We had a special ceremony with a Bishop present. During a Mass, the novice read out her vows to God, in the Brigidine way of life. When we were still Novices the first step was becoming Brides of Christ, but it is different now. After the first year in the Novitiate you were called a Postulant. Then at the end of that year, you asked permission of the Order to be allowed to become a Novice. The Postulant just wore a three-quarter black dress with a white collar and a little veil with hair showing. Novices had a black habit and a white veil. Upon taking the final vows, we dressed as brides and entered the church. There wasn't a husband in sight; there were nine brides when I took my vows! Ostensibly God, in the person of Christ, was the husband. We were all so young. I was 19. During the ceremony, your bridal attire was changed for a black monastic dress and veil. It was quite stark. Looking back, I think it was really quite hard on our families, because it was so stark. Thankfully, we don't wear those monastic clothes today.

Q: When you did take your final vows?

You became a Novice for two years and then at the end of that time you asked permission to take your vows for three years, initially, then for another two. At the end of this period you asked permission again to pledge your vows forever. The formal document of your Vows is signed by the Bishop and the Leader during a special ritual, called a Mass for Final Profession of Vows. For me this took placed in 1970.

Q: What was your feeling then when you were making that final commitment?

In a vague kind of way, I felt sure I was doing the right thing. It appealed to me and I had no doubts about it, but it has been lived out as I have tried to live out my life in subsequent years. It's probably a bit like marriage: you don't really know the full extent of what you are promising, but you know it's all the little things that come after, that makes it real. That's how I see it.

Over the years I suppose my approach to spirituality has changed. My image of God has changed as well. I see God as all around us in people and nature and within us. Earlier, it was easy to pray for things to happen and to pray to a God who was out there somewhere, but I don't think that any more. Now when someone asks me to pray for them, I don't find it difficult, because I just bring that person to mind and wish what is best for them. My own approach to the Divine is that divinity is all around us. My spirituality is pretty simple really.

Q: Do you find that your relationship with God has deepened through your life of serving?

Yes, I think it has. Jesus means a lot to me, his life and what He said. I find that a lot of trappings set up by the Church institution do not matter anymore. I believe that we should get back to what Jesus was about, and make the institutions more recognisable to what he taught.

Q: What are your future plans?

I probably haven't got a great big plan for the future. I'm 72 now, but I really don't think about when to stop working. There are still loads of needs in our world today. Fortunately, I'm reasonably healthy, so I can plan to keep doing what I can. In terms of work at the Centre, my plan is to find other people who can facilitate the programs we want to offer here. I really love teaching, and I don't miss teaching students. I find it life-giving when people who are disillusioned with the Church come here, and they are able to participate in programs. Many actually say that this is where they find church. In other cases you see the sorrow in people who are grieving the loss of a beloved partner, eventually coming back to life again. When I first took up the Coordinator position of Kildara Centre I thought, "We're dealing mainly with people my age; they're all older retired people." I used to think we should be doing something for younger people. That doesn't bother me now. The older people need something as well. I find Kildara Centre to be very life-giving, for me, and for those who come here.

Catriona's recipe on next page.

Vegetable Rissotto (Vegetarian)

Serves 8

INGREDIENTS

125g butter
2 onions
2-3 cloves garlic, finely chopped
1 cup zucchini, diced
1 cup carrot, diced
1 tin diced tomatoes
1 cup green peas, fresh or frozen
1 cup of any mixture of other vegetables in season, diced
2 cups dry white wine
500g arborio rice or barley
6 cups of vegetable or chicken stock
½ cup grated romano cheese
Ground black pepper

METHOD

1. Divide the butter into four equal pieces. Melt one piece in a saucepan and gently cook half the onions and garlic.
2. Add the vegetables and gently stir fry, adding 1 cup of wine gradually. Cook until all the liquid has evaporated. Put a lid on this and set aside.
3. In another saucepan, melt two pieces of the butter and add the remaining onion and garlic and cook until the onion is soft. Add rice and stir until it is well coated with the butter.
4. Add the remaining cup of wine and stir until the wine has been absorbed.
5. In a separate saucepan, boil the stock and gradually stir into the rice mixture until each cupful has been absorbed. In about 20-25 minutes the rice should be cooked and should be tender and creamy.
6. Stir in the remaining butter, the vegetable mixture and half the cheese.
7. Season to taste with freshly ground pepper.
8. Serve at once, with the remaining cheese. Serve with hot crusty bread rolls and a bottle of chilled chardonnay.

Gai Scrivens - A Walk with Nelson Mandela

Gai Soorjee is my maiden surname and Scrivens is my married surname. I have had experiences which have been just exceptionally phenomenal in my lifetime. I don't know my Dad; I've never met him. He passed on when I was little. I have three mothers, a Jewish mother, an Indian mother and a Catholic mother who is also Indian. I found this very interesting in my life. I was born in Mafeking, South Africa.

When I was three years old, I was hit by a motor car that crossed from one side of the road to the other. I was left totally unconscious and people thought that I had died. I was told that a monkey ran down from the roof of somebody's home and picked me up. The monkey actually gave me her milk to get me going again. She held me so tightly and wouldn't let me go until the ambulance arrived. The monkey gave me to the ambulance driver and then went back onto one of the roofs. I was told this story when I was six years of age. When I recovered, I was taken away and went to live with my Jewish Mom. My Jewish mother was so protective of me and told people not to come into her home with any negativity; no negative thoughts or negative talk. She wanted me to get well and move on in life. Of course, that is what happened. She sent me to school and I got my education and I did what I had to do as any child did. At the age of twelve, I got involved in politics and I had to leave South Africa two years later. The only way for me to leave was to get under a truck and go to Botswana and get my freedom there.

It was such a story that it makes you wonder. From one instant there is a child who has been hit by a car, is almost dead and told that she is not going to live. You've got broken bones and you won't survive. You'll be in a wheelchair and this is it, it's the end. Then you grow up and you find that your parents' property was taken away and you decide to get into politics and fight back to take the land back. I was given to understand that my mothers toiled and worked hard to get that land to grow fruit and vegetables so that they could achieve sustainable living. There were no handouts from the government, so my mothers decided to provide a living that way.

I grew up and got involved in politics to fight for freedom in South Africa and then I had to leave the country very quickly at a young age. To travel from South Africa to Botswana, I got under a truck. I hid by lying flat underneath the truck; I was fourteen years old. I stayed there for a little while until my mothers could get to me. And then I thought, "Well, I'll travel around that area, move around and see what's happening," because there was no work and they wouldn't employ a child. That was the sad part. One day in Botswana, I was walking towards a river and met a pastor. I was going to sit at the side of the river and contemplate where am I going from here? I knew there was a supreme being above and I thought that really, he's got to guide me. He's got to tell me where, what and how. I came from a very spiritual background, there was always God instilled in my life. No matter which religion, which ethnic group, race, creed or colour, God was always instilled in us. When I say us, I had a foster brother as well, so we grew up together. When I was sitting at the river, a big cloud of dust suddenly swooped and my eyes were full of sand. As I was rubbing the sand out of my eyes, I felt something touching my shoulder and I heard, "You'll be okay. Girl, you'll be okay." I couldn't open my eyes properly, so I scooped some water out of the river and washed my eyes. When I looked up, all I could see was white cloud, it was absolutely white. I felt, "You're going to be fine," and I laughed. I started laughing non-stop and believe you me, still today when I start laughing I will laugh non-stop. I just love laughing. When this happened I thought, "But why am I laughing? I don't know where I'm going from here. I'm living with people that I don't even know. I don't know how am I going to get from point A to point B. I haven't got any money in my pocket. I've left my mothers. They don't know where I am. How are they going to contact me? What's going to happen?" I decided to say a prayer. I was laughing and calmed down and said a prayer. Then a light shone – just like that. All I heard myself say was, "Thank you, God." That's all I heard myself say. I actually wrote this down in my diary to remember the time when it happened. I just burst out crying after that; I cried and I cried and I felt okay and I started walking again. I walked towards the house where I lived, and when I got to the house there was a parcel from my Jewish Mom. How? Where? There was no detail or anything on the parcel, but the parcel arrived. Even the people in the house couldn't understand it. They said to me, "Did you give our address to anybody? Do you know what's going to happen if the South African Government knows where we are?" Then it dawned on me that nobody was supposed to know. But I didn't tell anybody, I really didn't tell anybody. Later, after I opened the parcel, there was an envelope with money in it. It came with a different truck driver than the one who brought me to Botswana and was delivered to this home. My Jewish mother had contacted some of the truck drivers because they would help people escape when anything happened. My mothers contacted the different truck companies and found out where I was dropped off and that's how my Jewish mother sent me the parcel with money, clothes and a ticket to leave Botswana for the United Kingdom. Three days later, I left Botswana; I was fourteen years old. I lived in the United Kingdom for eight years. Whilst I was there, I got in touch with government embassies and spoke to them about the situation in South Africa.

When I arrived in Heathrow Airport, I didn't know where I was going; there was no accommodation or anything arranged. I had 500 Rand in my pocket. A lady at the airport reception told to me about an inexpensive motel not far from the centre of London and she gave me all the maps. My three mothers had arranged if anything I needed required money, it was to be given to me by a particular person and with that money I was to find work, educate myself and study. Study, work and holiday. I remember the first day when I went to Hyde Park from the airport. I was looking for Piccadilly Circus because I wanted to go to the circus. I was asking people, "I need to go to the big tent called Piccadilly Circus. Where is the circus? Please let me know." Everybody looked at me as if to say you're so stupid, we've got no circus here, we haven't got a big tent here. But nobody's telling me there's no circus. One lady came to me; she must have been in her 40s and explained that I was standing on the corner of Piccadilly Circus. I asked, "No animals?" She burst out laughing; really she did. She said, "Come on, where do you want to go to?" So I replied, "Well, I thought there was a circus so that I could just go and relax and decide what I want to do." She asked me, "Where are you staying?" I said, "Well, I'm at a motel in Hyde Park."

I thought this is good; I'm all by myself, I've got nobody to tell me what to do, I am the boss. I am really the boss. The following day I had a phone call from a company called British Home Stores and I was offered a job in the wages and salaries department of British Home Stores. How it was arranged until this day I don't know, I can't tell you how it was done. The lady who interviewed me told me to come to the office at such and such a time tomorrow and this is how you're going to start. In those days, the work was done manually on index cards. That was my first office job. How exciting, I tell you. The British Council gave me the opportunity to do an extra course in accountancy for a month in either Italy or Paris, so I chose Paris. I could work, I could holiday and I could study. Of course, I wanted to go to France and see Paris. At my age I had heard so much about it. This was so exciting and I thought, "Wow, what a life at the age of 14. Wow, girl, move." I had to learn a few things relating to accountancy first; this is what the British Council paid for. I ended up studying for three months before going to Paris for a month.

Back in the United Kingdom, I spent a whole year doing a bit of studying, a bit of work and then I decided I'll go and look for a part-time job because I wasn't too happy with handouts. I decided I'm going to look for a part-time job at the student council. I went to the student council and applied for a job at the café. There was table tennis, karate and everything happening there and I thought, "This is amazing, wow, this is heaven." So I decided to study accountancy there and that's what I did. I lived in the United Kingdom for a further eight years. While I was studying I decided it was time to move on my own. "I've had the help, next year I'm turning 15 and then I need to do something very constructive with my life." But, of course politics came between my plans again and it was hell to pay. It was hell to pay because people contacted me. I had the contacts, I had to get to the South African Embassy and speak to people there. I didn't have a clue how to address these things, but I had to go and do it. I was the youngest and I could get away with things at that point in time. People would listen to me because I was a child figure. I would get messages and letters from Botswana; go and do this, go and speak to this one, go and speak to that one. Then I thought, "Well, politics is very interesting, I'll throw everything aside and I'll get involved in politics." That was the biggest mistake I made. Then I decided to stay in the United Kingdom, go back to Botswana after four years, and then go back again to the United Kingdom. So after four years I went back to Botswana. I wanted to thank the people in Botswana, because there was no time to really thank them when I left. It was as if I was pushed from side to side; as if something was pushing me in a certain direction. I felt that I had to do this and I had a duty to fulfil. I have to go to these people, thank them for their time and everything that they've done for me.

I went to Botswana and my mothers came from South Africa to meet me. They said to me, "You're not staying in South Africa; you've got to go back; there's no way that you're going to be able to live here, you must go back." I said, "But I want to be at home." They replied, "No, you haven't got a home here, there's no home. There's no home for you, you've got to go back to the United Kingdom, you are settled there, you're working, you're studying, so you've got to carry on with your life." After two months, I went back to the United Kingdom. I studied and worked and decided to travel the world while living in the United Kingdom. I met a German friend, Ursula, and we went hitchhiking throughout Europe. In every country we met different people, we would make a group and move from one place to another. Ursula and I hitchhiked together for two years. It was exciting. We would stop at a place to work and make money. I knew hairdressing, so I would look for jobs. We would wash dishes in restaurants if we wanted to have a plate of food and didn't have enough money. We would tell the managers in the restaurant that we would clean up the kitchen and the restaurant, and that was the form of payment for a meal; we would move on.

Eventually this came to an end and I decided I'm going back to Bophuthatswana, South Africa, the area where I originated from. Then I decided to start my own business by manufacturing and designing furniture. While in France, I did a course in interior decorating, curtaining and gold gilding. I thought I could make money with this and that's how I started my business. When I returned to Mafeking, I got the government to open a small industry complex for small industries. I occupied a 1,000 square metre building and employed 125 people, and taught them how to hold a hammer and knock a nail in. I thought, this is great! But, of course, when Mandela was released from prison that's when trouble started again; I got involved again and I had to leave in a hurry.

The German friend I hitchhiked with was now living in Perth, Australia. She always used to say to me to come to Australia, and I would say no. I also had an uncle who came from Scotland and now lived in Sydney. The day I was going to come to Australia to meet him and live with him, we got the message that he had passed away; he was 92. I thought, "What on earth? I'm not going to Australia anymore because he's passed away." I thought, "Well, in any case, maybe I should go." My friend, Ursula, put an advertisement in a church magazine. Peter, my husband, went to church that particular week, after a very long time on in attendance. The priest came from the podium and gave Peter the magazine and said, "Take this, go home and tell me in a month's time if it has served your purpose." Within two weeks, Peter went back to thank the priest. He said it served his purpose immediately. Two years prior to this, Peter had lost his wife due to cancer.

Soon after, Peter called me in South Africa and that's how I met my husband. It was as if God's hand was there all the time. I knew I was being guided; there were mishaps, but I overcame them. There were blockages and hurdles to jump over, but I got over them. I climbed the mountains and I fell down; I got up and I climbed, then again I got up and I climbed. Eventually I climbed and went one way, and here I am in Australia with a wonderful husband and wonderful people like you around me. Isn't that fantastic? When Peter contacted me he said to me, "I'm sending you a ticket. Please come over." I said, "No, I've got a business and I can't leave." He said, "Alright. Just come and have a look." I had never met Peter and I thought, "Well, here's my opportunity to go to Australia, I'll go and see; I still have my business, I still have everything." I had nothing to lose. I thought that if I didn't like the place, I would just come back to South Africa because I had my house and my business. When I arrived Peter, waited for me at the airport. I had never seen him, but I went straight to him and tapped him on the shoulder and said, "Hello, Peter. I'm Gai". He said, "Yes. The voice tells me it's you. How did you know I was standing here?" It was my spiritual guidance that took me to him and brought me this far all my life. Peter asked my hand in marriage and I said, "I'll have to think about it." I went back to South Africa; I looked at my business, I looked at my house and I said, "I'll go," and I left everything. I just left it and I walked away. It was as though I was told don't take anything. When I came back to Australia, Peter said, "We'll have to ship everything to Australia." But by the time we decided to do this, there was nothing left of my business or my house; everything was plundered and taken. It was just too heart-breaking, all my hard work, I lost everything. I lost a fully paid house and my vehicles. I lost everything, but I don't regret it today, because these are material things in life. I have my sanity and I have all the love around me, that's more important.

Question: Tell us about your work with Nelson Mandela.

Gai: You're going to make me cry now. You're going to make me cry, it's like a lump gets in my throat. The political side is a very hard one for me now. I used to lobby for Nelson Mandela while he was in prison. Because I lived in Mafeking, I decided to print pamphlets at my business and distribute them in South Africa. Mafeking was in Bophuthatswana, which was not part of South Africa at that time, so I could more easily print the pamphlets without detection. Nelson Mandela was due to come out of prison the following year. There was a very close friend of mine who was a solicitor, in fact he passed away four years ago. He said to me, "If anything happens on the road just let me know," because he was also fighting for Nelson Mandela at that time.

I drove my ute to deliver the pamphlets in what was then called the North West Province. I was stopped at road blocks in Lichtenburg and Ventersdorp, both Afrikaner areas. Eugène Terre' Blanche, (who was murdered) held an AK47 right against my head and ordered me out of the vehicle. I had one of my workers next to me and I said to him, "Phineas, get out of the car on the other side and just stand that side, because they can hurt you and I'll do all the answering." He still said to me, "I can't leave you alone." I said, "No, I'll be okay, don't worry." The pamphlets on the car seat were covered, but the ones on the floor were not. The Afrikaners were busy searching vehicles to find people supporting Nelson Mandela come out of prison. They were looking into the vehicle and looking at the pamphlets, but couldn't see a thing. As I was getting out of the ute, Eugène Terre' Blanche was still holding the AK47 at my head. He shut the door and said, "Give me the keys." I gave him the keys. The Afrikaners went inside the ute and looked; they couldn't pick out anything, that's how I got through. What covered me in that situation was God's spirit. This is how I look at it. God put a blind down so that they didn't see the pamphlets. They looked at me and said in Afrikaans, "Gaan verby jou koelie meid," meaning get through, you bloody Indian. That's what they said in their language. They said it more harshly, I don't want to use the language they used. I just prayed and I drove through. My worker who was sitting next to me came and held my hand and said to me, "You are so strong; you are so strong." You know, I can still hear his voice. I said, "We are out, let us go now, we can go back to work." When I got to the other side, at the first church I came to, I got out of the vehicle, went inside and said, "Thank you God, I'm safe." That's what I did. That's how I got through. I delivered all the pamphlets, did what I had to do and came back to Mafeking three days later. Of course, when Nelson Mandela came out of prison, he couldn't thank us enough because he heard what was happening while he was in prison. He was told everything that was happening.

I witnessed whatever Winnie, Mandela's ex-wife, did. We were part of it, because her lover, who was the doctor murdered by Winnie's bodyguard, was actually related to one of my friends. So it was a very close connection. My mothers had very close contact with Nelson Mandela as well, and when he was in prison, they were being watched all the time. That's why, when I was 14, my mothers felt that if they send my foster brother and me away, then they can do what they have to do. They died fighting in any case. When Nelson Mandela came out of prison, he didn't even get to see them.

You felt forced to get involved in the battle to break down apartheid, otherwise you've had it. Today, even though people fought for a better South Africa, it has become ten times worse, because now it's reverse apartheid. That's what's happening now, it's reversed. The sad part was, I think people were hoping that when Mandela would come out of prison they'll be able to do A, B, C and D. It was nothing like that. What actually happened was people who fought at the grassroots, I was one of them, eventually got pushed to the side and those who took power threw everybody else who worked at grassroots down the drain. They did; we did the dirty work and the people who took power reaped the benefits. Today you find, especially with the coloured and the Indian children, they haven't got the privileges that they used to have when it was under white rule. The Indian communities have to open their own schools. The government believed that the Indian people are rich, that they have money, so they must open up their own businesses. They were not getting employed anywhere.

Desmond Tutu put a lot of work into reconciliation. He was talking about forgiveness and including everybody in the process. But it hasn't happened up until today. Nobody will tell me otherwise. Tutu is fighting, because a lot of the people are against him for seeking reconciliation. It's been very hard for him; at this stage he can't do much. His health is not permitting it either, because he has cancer as well. As much as he can say, he will say. But there isn't much that he can do. When he was younger, they would get together, have meetings and mobilise people. He can't do that anymore.

There were many big, beautiful homes that have been taken away from the people who left South Africa. Businesses were taken away, and when people went back to South Africa to go back to their homes and their businesses, they were mobbed. They just had to leave and get out. I met a couple not so long ago speaking Afrikaans in a shopping centre and I thought, "That's strange, it's the first time in Australia that I hear somebody speak Afrikaans." I went up to the lady and I greeted her in Afrikaans. She was so surprised. We chatted and she told me that the farm her parents had, was taken, and the house that her parents were living in, was burnt. Her parents were also taken away. They went to Kenya and they thought they could go back, but they couldn't. They ended up in Harrismith, which is halfway to Durban, and were both killed on a farm there. She was actually sobbing when she was telling me the story.

So, yes, I walked the walk with Nelson Mandela, I did walk the walk with him. That's just a little bit of the story. Today I think that's why I have the attitude; whatever happens in life, for every bad thing in life, there's ten good things ahead. Our whole life, irrespective of who you are or what you are, our life is a spiritual journey; every day is a spiritual journey. Really, I don't believe in negatives, saying this is not going to work or that is not going to work. There's a reason why it won't work, because there's ten positive things ahead. That's why you must not feel upset; good things will happen. Whatever happens in life, there's a reason for it. There's ten good things ahead, it's waiting. You'll reap the benefit.

Today I'm a happy woman, happily married and not even concerned about what I've lost in South Africa. I've lost millions. I always tease my husband and I say to him, "I've come to poverty pastures, darling," and he says, "I know." The important thing is I'm happy; I don't care about what I've lost, it's one of those things.

That's my spiritual journey.

Vegetable Patties with Chutney

Serves 2

INGREDIENTS

2 cups fresh mixed vegetables or 1 cup mixed frozen vegetables
1 onion grated
½ teaspoon green ground chillies
½ teaspoon ground garlic
Chopped coriander
Dhania Jeeru Indian spice to taste (see below for the recipe)
Turmeric - pinch
Salt to taste
3 potatoes boiled in jackets and mashed
2 eggs beaten
Breadcrumbs

METHOD

1. Braise onions in butter or ghee just until the onions are soft.
2. Add spices and vegetables and stir fry until all moisture has evaporated.
3. Allow to cool.
4. Mix together the vegetables, coriander, spices, salt and mashed potatoes. Form spoonfuls of the mixture into patties.
5. Dip the patties in the beaten egg mixture, followed by the breadcrumbs.
6. Fry slowly in very little oil, moderately hot until golden brown and crispy.
7. Drain on paper towel.
8. Serve hot with chutney.

Dhania Jeeru Indian spice

INGREDIENTS

1 cup coriander seeds
½ cup cumin seeds
1 cinnamon stick
1 ½ tbsp whole black pepper
2-3 cloves

METHOD

1. Keep Coriander and cumin seeds in sunlight for 1 hour.
2. Combine all the ingredients and grind them to a fine powder.
3. Dhania Jeeru Powder is ready to use. Keep it in a dry airtight jar.

Audry Hurley - Doves of Peace

I am very honoured to be given this opportunity to tell my story, because now I'm at the end of my life, having an incurable disease and spending a lot of my time in bed; sometimes so out of breath that I can't speak when I want to. To be asked to speak to you is really quite an honour and it's very exciting. My name is Audry Hurley, and my story is connected to doves. I had an idea a long time ago to release white doves at weddings. In the beginning, when I started releasing doves at weddings, I was asked by a group of women to share my dreams and what doves at weddings are all about, because no-one had heard about releasing doves at weddings at that time. The Doves of Peace started with me sharing this ritual with a group of women. The dove is a symbol of peace and women are the nurturers and the purveyors of peace, so it seems natural that I would start with sharing my story connected to the doves.

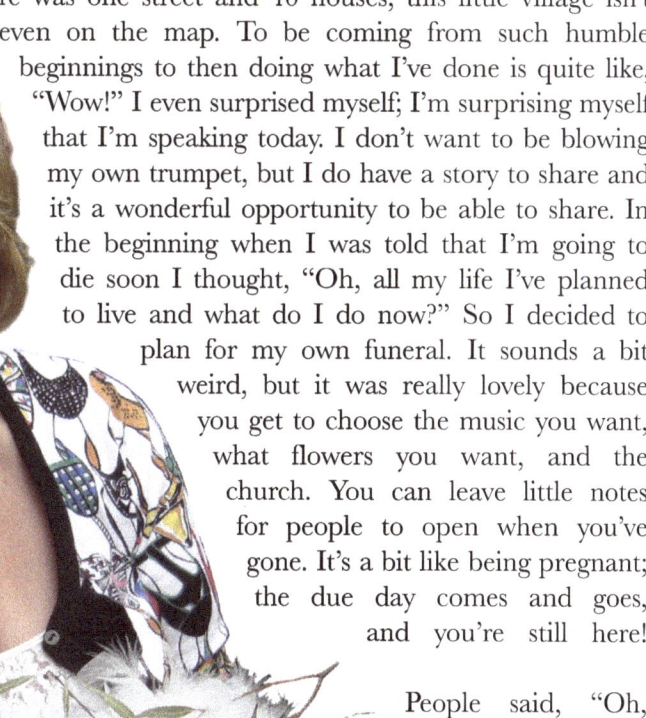

I was born in a very tiny, rural village in Lincolnshire, England. At that time, there was one street and 40 houses; this little village isn't even on the map. To be coming from such humble beginnings to then doing what I've done is quite like, "Wow!" I even surprised myself; I'm surprising myself that I'm speaking today. I don't want to be blowing my own trumpet, but I do have a story to share and it's a wonderful opportunity to be able to share. In the beginning when I was told that I'm going to die soon I thought, "Oh, all my life I've planned to live and what do I do now?" So I decided to plan for my own funeral. It sounds a bit weird, but it was really lovely because you get to choose the music you want, what flowers you want, and the church. You can leave little notes for people to open when you've gone. It's a bit like being pregnant; the due day comes and goes, and you're still here!

People said, "Oh, I didn't expect to see you! How are you?"

Then, five years later, they're still saying that. Oh, my goodness, now it's become a joke. I've been through the planning to die bit. I thought, "Well, I haven't died, clearly; so I may as well stand up and plan to live." I'm on the journey now, of planning to live again. I find that I can still do things; even though I can't physically do them, I can still learn lots of things. I can reminisce, I can remember and I can share some of the highlights of my journey, which have been very spiritual, emotional and exciting.

In my business, I've had to learn to be the graphic art designer, the receptionist and the promoter. At wedding receptions, I presented the doves to be released to the bridal couple. I would walk down the catwalk with the doves and give the doves to models. I've been to weddings where there've been snake charmers, belly dancers, drummers and people swallowing fire or swords. The dove is a symbol all around the world, in all cultures and all religions. So I had the opportunity to attend different celebrations and that became very, very exciting. I've released the doves at peace protests and ceremonies to commemorate 50 years of peace after World War II.

When I first came over to Victoria from England, I came over with my three boys. I had a little job in the kindergarten in Healesville looking after autistic children at the Living and Learning Centre. When I was looking after the children, I had an accident where I fell down suddenly. I had a back operation and so it was difficult to continue to work there. At around the same time, I caught a disease called psittacosis, which is a bird disease. Really, I had never had anything to do with birds, ever, so it was a bit of a mystery. It seemed that all the birds flying around in the wild somehow scattered their disease on me, and I was the one who got the bird disease. I ended up in Fairfield Hospital and was feeling very, very poorly for about three weeks. When I came out of hospital, a girlfriend invited me to a party where I met a man who owned a bird shop. Silly me – I thought that was some sign; I'd caught a bird disease, which is bizarre, and then I met a man with a bird shop. I used to go to the bird shop and loved it – all the little bird noises; it was very, very soothing for me. The owner said to me one day, "What if you bought the bird shop?" I didn't know anything about birds, except that they didn't have hairy legs and they had beaks. That was about it! The owner said that the bird shop would be a good little job for my boys and that he would train them to run the business. I asked my middle son and my youngest son what they thought, and they thought it was not a bad idea. We decided to buy the bird business, but within a week, the guy (owner) left; so we ended up with a bird business, knowing nothing whatsoever, about birds. It happened that the customers taught us everything we needed to know. How we managed to keep the doors open, I don't know, but we did. I started going to the sale yards to buy birds; that was very interesting because the people there taught me about pigeons. They would tell me funny stories about the dove being the original messenger. Friends of Melbourne jail inmates would put $20 in a ring band placed on the pigeon's leg. The bird would then fly to the Melbourne jail, and the inmate would take the money so that he or she could buy their cigarettes. They would also send little messages. It was probably where I got my bird disease from, because the whole room would be thick with feathers and dust. But, I learnt the tricks of the trade.

One day (in my 40s), I was driving to the airport to collect some birds. At an intersection on Bell Street there was a traffic jam made up of wedding cars. Beside me was a white limousine and on the other side a black limousine. At the adjacent side of the traffic lights were coaches and horses. The bridal parties were crisscrossing at the lights and it was just really lovely. I remember thinking to myself, "Oh, what a lovely industry this would be. What could I do to be in this industry?" It sounds silly, but a voice came down into the car and bellowed in my ear: you can do doves. And I remember saying, "Yes, I can do doves." So, when I got home I said to my three teenage boys that I'd had this voice from God and that I could do doves at weddings. I didn't get a very positive response! I wasn't going to be denied this venture, I was just so excited and I was going to do it. My son said to me, "Mum, what do you know about weddings?" I said, "Well, nothing." He said, "Okay, how many weddings have you been to since you've been in Australia for 20-odd years." I said, "Well, I haven't been to any, because you guys are boys and you haven't got married, and we'd moved around and what has that got to do with it?" He said, "Mum, you need to know a little bit about weddings. How much money are you going to invest in this new business of yours, what sort of capital?" So I said, "Well, I don't have any; you know I don't have any." So he said, "Okay, here we are struggling with this business and you want to start another business?" I said, "Yes." He said, "No, I don't think so. What do you know about advertising, because the bridal industry is all about advertising?" I replied that I didn't know about that either. Then he said, "Oh well, that should tell you that it's not a very good idea."

On the Monday, I registered the name and started the business, Wedding Bell Birds, and I have been on this lovely journey ever since. It's just been amazing. I found that all sorts of people help you. For instance, you can go to the advertising magazines, and the graphic art designers will put something together for you because he wants his magazine to look okay, so he'll do it for you. I advertised, got the bookings and then payed the advertiser; it did turn out to be a bit of a circle, but that's what I did and I enjoyed it. We've had funny weddings. Once we were to release 15 white doves at a wedding, so it was very spectacular. We were told the St. James Church was in Carlton and the wedding was at 1.30pm. My husband, John, and I went to Carlton, but there wasn't a St James in Carlton, so we looked around Brunswick, No, there wasn't one there either. I ran into the police station and asked if they could tell me where St. James was. It was in Reservoir, which was kilometres away. I had a telephone number. I called and spoke to the grandfather who had a thick accent and he said, "Oh, she is only just leaving." When we got there, the bride had been very, very late and the service had been very, very long. We were waiting for about half an hour and they came out of the church; the bride was about nine months pregnant and her bouquet was long, very elaborate and expensive. The groom was really good-looking and quite wealthy. The bride had a great big, triumphant smile! Her smile said, "All you girls missed out, you missed it. I got it!" The whole adventure was very funny; we laughed about that.

I'll tell you about my own wedding, because that was very exciting. John and I went to the church that we thought we would get married in, but the pastors and priest all said no, we can't marry you, because John's a divorced Roman Catholic and I'm a divorced Anglican girl. Therefore, John and I decided that we'd get married on top of Mount Donna Buang; we had a beautiful wedding. I had a cathedral-type birdcage dress with dove images with fantails on it. In the rescue hut on top of the mountain we had a log fire burning, and in the square outside, we held the ceremony. Because we were married on the 1st May, we had a maypole and guests did maypole dancing. The cake even had fantail doves on the icing. The whole theme was doves, doves and doves. John and I were members of Toastmasters. Toastmaster members were singing old, English folk songs, and it was very, very exciting. For our wedding holiday, we went to China because I could go to the bridal exhibitions. We had banquets and feasts and we climbed the Great Wall. But, we weren't going to franchise our business in China. They wanted my business and for us to pay them – I think it was $50,000.

John and Audry's wedding day.

There was a girl who had breast cancer and she died. I went to release a dove for her courage outside the church. They were playing 'Wind beneath my wings' as she came out, so I knew releasing the doves was right. It was a great big media event with cameras everywhere. As the coffin was put in the hearse, I released a dove over the coffin. A photograph was taken and appeared on the front page of the newspaper. People said to me, why don't you do doves at funerals as well? It became a good marriage – we did funerals during the week and weddings on the weekend. Then we decided to change the name of the business to Doves of Peace.

We met Hazel Edwards who wrote Hippopotamus on my roof; she's written over 100 children's books. I took her to the auction market where I used to buy and sell birds, and I showed her how the bird business worked. Hazel wrote a children's book about Serena; my first fantail dove named Serena. In the story, Serena was stolen by some people and was going to be used for a wedding on Saturday. The story was all about the shop, myself and my doves. It was quite a privilege.

Some of the funerals that we've done have been amazing. I've done some mafia-type funerals. Once, I'm sure I saw a gun in the overcoat pocket of one gangster at a funeral for his mum. One really powerful funeral was for a three-year-old boy. A man in his 30s came with a police escort; he was in handcuffs. He knelt down, I gave him the dove and then he released the dove over the grave of his son. The father had picked up his son from his Mum's home and taken him to the milk bar, but he didn't put the seatbelt on, and now the little boy was dead. It was really, really, really sad. These are the situations that you know the doves can heal people. When we did the Port Arthur massacre funerals, Sarah, the mother of a 16-year-old girl could hardly stand up. She was so depressed and when she released a dove, I could see the bird heal her. She released the dove standing up by herself, whereas before, people needed to help her stand up. She said, "This is for you, Sarah." Wow, that's something real. At another funeral where a man lost his wife and two girls, as he released three doves, one flew up, came back down and walked around his legs. He said to us, "My wife just wanted to say goodbye to me."

These precious memories stay with you, and I knew I was on the right track. In life, if you can find something that can give people some joy and happiness, or peace and comfort, then you're on the right road. I feel that my spiritual journey has been a really good one, and I've learnt a lot from it. I think that the dove is an art form, so whichever way you look at the dove, it's going to give beauty. When you see something beautiful it's never lost, because it goes in your heart and stays in your memory forever. Now I feel that I've pretty much come full circle; I've done what I wanted to do. Now I'm in another stage of my life that I don't know what's going to happen; but seeing that I'm now on the road to living, I just have to wait and see what can come up next.

Thank you for allowing me to share with you. I am thankful for the opportunity of having the doves; they are the messengers to share my story. Thank you.

Audry passed away in the summer of 2016 surrounded by her husband, John, and her loving family. We are so grateful to have had the opportunity to share and record Audry's journey.

Elsie's Plum Bread

Serves 8

INGREDIENTS

500g self-raising flour
500g plums (or mixed fruit)
225g butter
¾ cup brown sugar
1 tbsp treacle
1 cup water

METHOD

1. Warm the butter until it melts.
2. Let the butter cool slightly, then pour it into the mixing bowl onto the flour.
3. Add the eggs and mix together.
4. Add the fruit, treacle and water; mix well.
5. Pour the total mixture into 2 well-greased & lined tins (1kg size).
6. Bake for 2 hours in the oven: for the 1st hour bake at 150 degrees Celsius, for the 2nd hour bake at 135 degrees Celsius.

Beth Treacy - A Jewish girl

My name is Beth Treacy. I was born in New Jersey, USA in 1953 within a Jewish family. I'm the middle child, and I have an older brother and a younger brother; we're all two years apart. My parents were raised in Jewish homes; my mother's father came from Russia. My grandfather had a very thick, Russian, Yiddish accent. His name was Joseph, and my mother's mother had more of a Brooklyn accent. My father's grandfather was born in Russia. He passed away when my parents married in 1950, so I never met him; but he was the oldest child in a large family. He had five brothers and sisters; then his mother passed away and his father remarried; they had five more kids. My father's mother's name was Anna, and my grandfather's name was Edward. Anna's family came from Poland. We lived in the hometown of my father's family in New Jersey. My maiden name was Busch, but according to the tale I was told, the name wasn't Busch but the Russian name of Buschalavski. When my great grandfather arrived in America by boat and was processed on Ellis Island, the customs and immigration officials couldn't pronounce his name, so they anglicised it; that's where Busch came from. All the Buschs went to New Jersey. I remember my father's clan; there were so many uncles and aunties and cousins. We would gather together for a blessing over the wine with lots of cakes during Rosh Hashanah, the Jewish New Year; that's the only time I ever saw them.

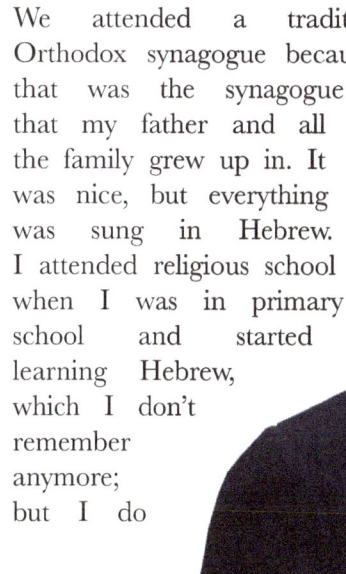

We attended a traditional Orthodox synagogue because that was the synagogue that my father and all the family grew up in. It was nice, but everything was sung in Hebrew. I attended religious school when I was in primary school and started learning Hebrew, which I don't remember anymore; but I do

Herstory

remember some of the basic prayers that are spoken. For instance, I remember the prayer over the bread and the prayer over the wine. The prayer to welcome in the Shabbat on Friday had a big impact on me, which is why all these years later, I can still remember it. I didn't have much interest in learning Hebrew, but my relationship with God and my spiritual journey, was definitely more spiritual or charismatic than Jewish. I wasn't entrenched in Judaism and there could be a few reasons for that. It could have just been my nature; but also, my parents weren't very religious even though they both came from Orthodox homes and did the traditional things such as going to synagogue on Friday and the High Holy Days. I think my parents became quite entrenched in materialism and success, especially my Dad. My father came from a poor family because his father was the oldest child of a big family and had no opportunity to study or develop himself. My grandfather had to work to support his extended family and siblings, and never had the opportunity to go to university. However, his younger brothers (my uncles) and my great uncles were able to become doctors, lawyers, accountants and whatever. My father's family was looked down upon by the rest of the family because they were poor. Because of that, my father had a tenacious drive to be successful, to have money and success. Making something of himself became his God and became his focus. Therefore, in terms of my own spiritual development and my belief in God, it was much more coming from within and wasn't anything that my parents taught me or talked to me about. Developing good character was never discussed.

Jewish people believe that they're the Chosen People, or they were chosen to receive the Messiah 2000 years ago. But that of course, didn't happen, and to this day, the Jewish people are still waiting for the first Messiah and they still believe that the Messiah is coming to them; I took issue with this point. I remember that I attended my cousin's Bar Mitzvah. A Bar Mitzvah is a special ceremony for a young 13-year-old boy to become a man. To complete this ceremony, boys study a portion of the Torah over six months. In the synagogue during the ceremony with the rabbi, the Torah is sung and read in Hebrew. After the celebration, the boy is considered a man and not a child anymore. During my cousin's Bar Mitzvah, I was 20 years old and I remember the rabbi talking about how the Jewish people are the Chosen People. I thought, "No, that's not right, I don't agree with that. I think all people are Chosen People." I didn't believe that the Jewish people were exclusively the Chosen People. When I was 12 or 13, my family moved to a Reform synagogue, which in Australia, is called Liberal Jewish. In Orthodoxy, the man always wears a hat, and the women wear long skirts. They're very traditional in that the women and children sit in a balcony up the back, and only the men can sit down in the main part of the synagogue and say the prayers with the rabbi. In the Reform synagogue, the families could sit together and the service was all in English. It gave a feeling of belonging, something I could relate to. I wasn't really religious, but I did feel connected with a certain culture. Most of my friends were Jewish, but I had a few Christian friends in high school. I went to the Jewish Youth Club and attended religious education on Sundays because Sunday is not the day of worship, Saturday is. Sabbath is the Saturday. I attended religious school and I really enjoyed it. The rabbi was a nice man; he had a young family and he was easy to relate to. From him, I felt something different; he wasn't so much about the Old Testament and the Torah, but about relevant things. For instance, when I was 15 or 16 and I remember we had a Friday night service where we sang a song from Peter, Paul and Mary, 'The great mandala.' The song is about peace and is very Zionistic about Israel. I remember the Six-Day War was taking place during that time and that we were doing things for Israel. So I was more Zionistic and not so spiritual or religious, but I had my own feelings about God.

I graduated from high school in year 12, and also graduated from religious education; I felt a certain accomplishment and closure. I went on to university, but struggled quite a lot. My parent's marriage was falling apart, and I didn't feel any spiritual nourishment from my family and I was wandering spiritually. I left university and didn't graduate, which was unfortunate as I look back. Then, I began to search and started doing transcendental meditation. I began looking more internally within, and reading Eastern religion books about the Hindu saints and Ramakrishna. I also read the Carlos Castaneda books about spiritual experiences through peyote mushrooms and astral projecting; Kahlil Gibran's book The prophet, and personal spiritual journeys of finding Nirvana with a cosmic consciousness and peace within myself; books about psychology and dealing with one's inner conflicts and struggles. I remember reading one book about narcissism. Narcissus is a Greek character who was totally self-absorbed and had too many conflicts inside. I identified certain things in the book about myself. I really believed in God, in the spiritual world and life after death, but I didn't follow Judaism. My path never took me to go to or join a Christian church. I had a friend in high school and I used to go with her to Midnight Mass at Christmas and I felt many things about Catholicism. I didn't have any feelings about Protestantism, but somehow I always wanted to be in the flock of Jesus. I didn't know what to do with it, because I didn't visit Christian churches, I was much more into Eastern religion, meditation and spiritual development and so on.

I left university in 1975 when I was 21, and worked in New York City for about a year in a clothing store in the retail fashion and merchandising industry. But I found it to be empty, dry and really a terrible environment. It didn't satisfy my spiritual thirst, so I quit that job and I moved up to Boston with my younger brother who was attending university up there. I rented a small room in a little boarding house around the corner from my brother who was living in an apartment with my cousin and a few others. I was doing transcendental meditation and reading so many books. A book that had an impact on me was The razor's edge, by Somerset Maugham. The young character in the book, Larry Darrell, really inspired me because he had a religious experience where he was searching for God. He went to India and his guru sent him up to meditate on a mountain top before dawn on his birthday. Just at the point where the dawn and the dark met, he felt an experience of amazing peace. He felt a cosmic consciousness of peace and total oneness of spirit and body and said to himself that if he died at that moment, he would die a happy man. It totally changed his life and gave him meaning to life; his life became a life of helping people and even people didn't understand him. This book brought about an awakening in me in that this is really what I wanted, to have that kind of peace and wholeness.

I was doing transcendental meditation and so on and keeping to myself, except for seeing my brother and my cousin. We were all working in a restaurant together. But I didn't have any kind of vision for my future and didn't think about plans. I didn't know what was happening and where my life was going to lead me; I was thinking more about spiritual things. My mother who had been suffering from manic depression for many years, she was not in a good way and my parents were divorced and it was always a big worry for me. In 1976, I went home over New Year's, and my mother was struggling a lot. I remember sitting down at the kitchen table. I prayed and I said to God, "Dear God, I really want to help my mother. Please show me what I can do. Amen." Our family was a skiing family, so after I saw my mother, my brother and my cousin and I, went to Vermont for a skiing holiday for a few days.

When I returned to Boston, I met a member of the Family Federation for World Peace and Unification (FFWPU) and was invited to the church centre. When I walked through the door, a feeling came over me; these are the people I've been looking for all my life. One of the ladies I'd seen in the bathroom library the day before and our eyes had met. I was looking at her, because she had really big, blue eyes that were very spiritual and I just kept staring at her eyes, but she didn't talk to me. Another time I was waiting for the tram to go home after work, and I was reading a newspaper call the East West Journal. It was a New Age newspaper and a young man started talking to me. We got on the tram and just before I got off the tram, one stop before his, he said, "My name is Tom Carter. I'm from the Unification Centre. Come by sometime." So, I thought, "Okay, where is that?" He didn't tell me where it was, but he planted a seed in my mind. When I walked in the door of the Centre, he was there and also the lady with the blue eyes. The funny thing is, the Unification Centre was just down the street from where I lived, and I walked by it every day near Kenmore Square. There was a big logo above the Centre and I walked by it so often and never noticed it, just two blocks from where I lived. God answered my prayers and showed me what I can do to help my mother. I had my own spiritual search and I was happy with that, but I could see how God was really working in my life. I heard the teachings and I was able to learn about Jesus and find a way to love and believe in Jesus through the Unification Church and through Rev. Dr. Sun Myung Moon. I was so grateful and felt that I could be in Jesus flock, understand the return of Christ at the Second Coming, and understand about True Parents. It was really a new life for me, and I did many different activities with the Church. I was on mobile teams, fundraising and working with the inter-religious and science conferences; it was an opportunity to meet many amazing people, even Nobel Prize winners. I realised that religion and science need each other, and this is what Rev. Moon was trying to instil in people through his teaching.

During the New Year's of 1980, I was able to meet my husband from Australia, Michael, through the engagement ceremony where Rev. Moon matched us together. I remember I looked at Michael; he was so tall, 6'5" (196cm) and I thought, "My gosh, he's so tall," because no-one in my family was tall at all; especially Eastern Europeans are tiny people. He's a very humble man, really loving, a good man who has been my pool of peace; I've learned so much from him and I'm grateful for him. In 1982, we went to the Blessing Wedding Ceremony in New York, and we have had five wonderful children and many wonderful experiences. We lived in Micronesia, a Pacific Island nation for four years between 2005 to 2009, which was a wonderful experience. I feel so grateful to have lived in a poor, developing country with Island people who have such a heart. We in Australia, have so much to learn from Island people. What we have is what they want; but actually, what we need is what they have – free hearts.

Treacy family September 2015

I realised that we need to bring

the world together and learn from each other because we're all 'one family under God,' and we're all the same. People have different external circumstances in where they live, but it doesn't change what's in their hearts, especially concerning issues around family and community.

Thank you very much.

Lemon Yoghurt Cake

This delicious, fragrant lemon yoghurt cake is so simple to make, and with no butter, it's a little healthier than your average dessert. This recipe is so versatile – you can experiment with different flavours of yoghurt, or even different citrus fruits for flavour combinations.

INGREDIENTS

1 cup sugar
½ tsp salt
2 eggs
3 tsp lemon juice
Zest of two lemons
¾ cup olive oil
1 cup natural yoghurt
2 cups self-raising flour

METHOD

1. Preheat your oven to 180°C.
2. In a bowl, mix the zest, oil, eggs and sugar with a fork.
3. Add the remaining ingredients and mix until well combined.
4. Pour the batter into a greased ring tin and bake for 30 minutes.
5. Remove the cake from the oven and allow to cool before turning out onto a serving plate.

Josephine Wane - Gratitude

My name is Josephine Wane, I'm from the Solomon Islands and visiting Australia for three months. I would like to talk about the path which I went through that enabled me to experience God's heart. I was born in a very humble family with a Christian background. My father and mother were both very strong Catholics. My father's lineage is very unique; I come from a very unique family. My father's mother was the only child in her family, and my father's father had three sons. When I was born, my father was very happy and celebrated my birth; he treated me well as the favourite child. In my family, I have two sisters and seven brothers; we have a very big family of ten children. When I grew up, I felt my father loved me so much; I felt like the queen in the family.

My father originated from Malaita, one of the major islands of the Solomon Islands. In the Malaita culture, girls are the ones who are treated as slaves to the family. Girls do everything; but my father didn't want my mother to treat me as though I was the slave to the family. When girls grow up and marry in the Malaita culture, they go to their husband. My mother was always concerned that if my father treated me like a queen, I wouldn't be a good wife to my husband: I would be a bossy mother and wouldn't respect the family I would go to in the future. My mother had a plan; she loves me a lot, but I never realised it. I thought my father loved me more than my mother, but my mother did love me equal to my father. They said they love every child equally, but that's how I felt towards my parents. After my father celebrated my birth, my parents never celebrated my birthday again.

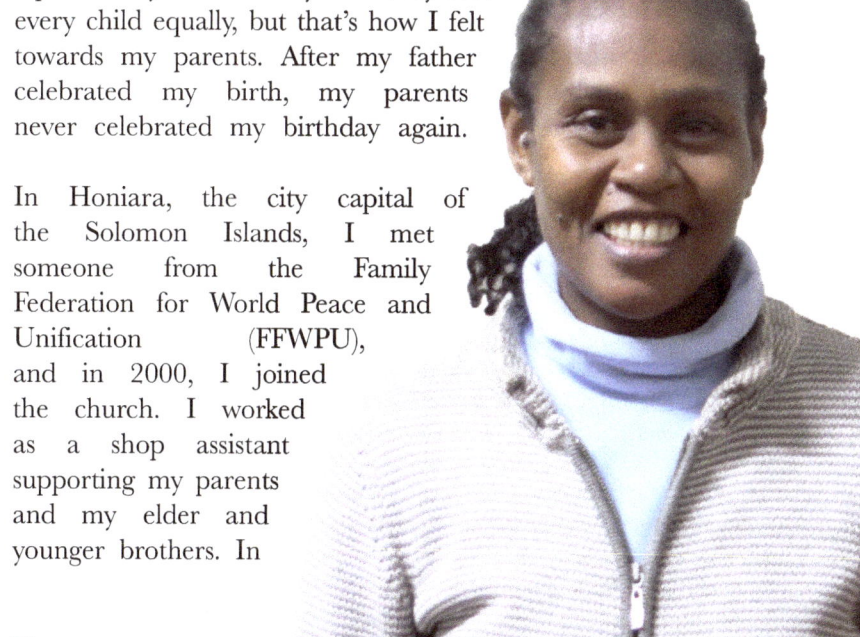

In Honiara, the city capital of the Solomon Islands, I met someone from the Family Federation for World Peace and Unification (**FFWPU**), and in 2000, I joined the church. I worked as a shop assistant supporting my parents and my elder and younger brothers. In

2001, I received the Marriage Blessing, and in 2002, I first visited Australia.

It was then that my parents first celebrated my birthday. I visited Sydney and also came here to Melbourne. I was inspired a lot because for the first time, I saw the 'second generation' in the church, and the children welcoming us to Australia. I went back to the Solomons in 2003, and then visited Korea and attended a 21-day women's workshop in Cheongpyeong. It was a good experience for me because it is a very special place. I want to always be in Cheongpyeong; it feels like heaven on earth. When I first entered the prayer hall, I experienced the feeling of missing my parents and then meeting them again. I experienced this when I left high school and first moved out from my parent's home. When I returned home and met my parents again, going to the prayer room felt like this. So yes, it is a very special place.

In 2004, I joined my husband. My first pregnancy was a miscarriage, and my heart was lonely to have a blessed child, as God's child. When I did give birth to my first daughter, I felt that God was alive and that He existed. At that time, both my husband and I worked in a public mission and had no money. Without even a cent, when I gave birth, everything was prepared for my daughter. Every church member, even though all of them had nothing, they prepared for my daughter's birth. Even though I had nothing, I could see that God really existed, and it was a miracle. My husband used to teach martial arts to the children of one of the Ambassadors for Peace, and before I gave birth, he gave us $2000 Solomon dollars. This was big money, and my husband never expected it. When I would say something about money, or tell him things about what we didn't have, he would say to me, "You have a wavering faith." So I just kept quiet and continued working in the mission. In 2005, Rev. Dr. Sun Myung Moon came to the Solomon Islands.

In 2008, my husband came to Australia. When he left, my two daughters and I stayed in the Church Family Centre on the east side of the main city in Honiara. He left us with nothing. All day I worked to survive, and sometimes, I locked my daughters in their room so I could work. I cooked banana chips, and then went to the market to sell all the products. I then came back, and they were still in their room all by themselves. One day when I came back, they were playing with medicine tablets. Usually I kept medicine tablets in a bag that I hung on a hook on the wall. This way, I could treat them when they got sick. I didn't realise that my girls could reach the bag. So when I came back from selling at the market on this day, they had taken the bag off the hook and taken the tablets out, broken them and were playing with them, but not eating them yet. Just when they started to taste the tablets, I opened the door. It was the right time. I opened the door and saw them playing with the tablets. I caught my daughter starting to taste the tablet by putting it on her tongue and she said, "Oh, it tastes like lollies." I opened the door and I saw that. Oh, my heart sank. It was just the right time because they hadn't taken the tablets yet. I took the tablets from them and threw them away. I realised, "Yes, God always guides me." When we experience life is tough, but we maintain our faith and believe in Him, He is always there when there is danger.

At that time, I was thinking, "What am I going to do? I cannot just stay like this, thinking only about my family, and just thinking about food every day." Every day, life seemed like the same circle – wake up, wash, prepare food, have breakfast and wait for lunch. All through the year, all through the months and the weeks and days, just like that. I was thinking that there is no use for me to be a missionary. Father Moon is telling us that we all have the responsibility to raise a nation for God. It is not an easy task, and I'm not an educated woman like others who have qualifications. So I was thinking, "What can I do to comfort God's heart?" In order to comfort God, it is always at the risk of life. I needed to do something because I was only focusing on my family. We were staying on the public church property and we were in debt. We had no money, nothing. So what could I do? I couldn't just stay like this, with no meaning to my existence.

In 2010, I came back to Australia to do some missionary work. But where could I leave my children? We had nothing. How could they survive? The week before my visa was accepted, my elder cousin volunteered to take care of my children, and she took care of them for the whole year. After the year was completed, I came back to the Solomons and saw my children. It was wonderful because when I left, they were like babies and did not want to go away from me. But when I came back, they had grown up much more, and they could take care of themselves. Before I left, my eldest daughter was shy and wanted to stay beside me rather than go in front with the other Sunday school children to sing during Sunday service. When I returned and saw her going out and singing with the other children, I was very happy. I thought, "Oh, that's how God works; she's growing up independent of me." I saw something different; I was very happy to see that they could do this.

During my one-year mission in Australia, I had a chance to meet my husband in Melbourne. I got pregnant, and went back to the Solomons with my son. During my time in Australia, I also went to Korea, to Cheongpyeong, and liberated all my ancestors and my husband's ancestors. I was very grateful to God, because He allowed me this very great experience. I stayed in the Solomons for four years. In 2014, I went back again to Korea for four months to raise funds for the Peace Embassy. Where there is a will, there is always a way, and my children were looked after again. When I came home, I was also very happy because I could see hope in my children. My youngest son stayed with Aunty Nelly and spoke to people in the same way that she did when selling to people in her shop. He always welcomed Nelly's customers, and when I took him back with me, the customers missed him.

Even though everything is difficult, I realise that that is life. If we are not going through sacrifices or tough things in life, then we never experience God's heart. When I experience difficulties, I really feel God's heart and feel God has trained me to become somebody who can show others the way when they are going through the same situations. So I am grateful to Heavenly Parents and Heavenly Father. Because of the path I went through, I realise who I am and what to do to help other women like me who've been through situations that they are finding difficult to overcome. I'm very grateful.

Thank you very much.

Cassava Pudding - A favourite of the Solomon Islands

Serves 8

INGREDIENTS

**1 kg cassava roots
500g brown sugar
2 cups coconut milk
2 eggs
85g butter
1 tsp cinnamon
1 tsp baking powder
1 cup hot water**

METHOD

1. Peel the cassava roots then rinse carefully and dry them.
2. Grate each section using a fine grater. Make sure to stop when you reach the stringy core. Do not use the core.
3. Combine the grated cassava, brown sugar, cinnamon, baking powder and coconut milk and mix well.
4. Add the eggs (previously beaten) and the melted butter. Mix thoroughly again.
5. While mixing the preparation continuously with a whisk, gradually pour hot water in the dough.
6. Pour into a buttered pan and bake in a preheated oven at 180C for about 45 minutes.
7. Cassava pudding should be golden brown. To test if done, gently shake the mold. The center should not be liquid or wobbly.
8. Once the cake is set, stop cooking so it does not dry out. Turn upside down and when cooled cut into cubes.

Peeled Cassava Root

Grated Cassava Root

Baked Cassava Pudding

Titilope Alao - Spirituality

I have changed my thinking pattern and I've succeeded in doing that; I just keep moving forward towards my goals using a holistic approach.

My home of origin is Lagos, Nigeria. I was born into a Muslim extended family. My parents were also raised by Muslims and my mum still practices as a Muslim. My Dad was also a Muslim but he converted into a Christian before he died and was buried as a Christian. He used to attend the Baptist Church and was laid down according to their principles. I never lived with both parents, I grew up with my mum so I used to follow her to the mosque whenever she was going. I used to pray in Arabic and read the Holy Koran as well, following her example. I did it really well. Anything I do, I really try to do it well. While growing up I went to a Catholic school and learnt how to pray in a Catholic way too. The catholic way of prayer became a part of me as well because our neighbours back in Nigeria were Catholics and they had a meeting prayer in front of their house once a week and I would sit down looking down from our balcony and prayed along with them. While I was growing up, I visited both the Mosque and the Church. I attending Church was also influenced by my neighbours, it wasn't really my dad that influenced me but both my mum and dad had no problem with that. The interesting thing is that, whatever church I visited, I did it well. I was a good Muslim and a good Christian which was part of my personal moral, to be the best at anything I did. Sometimes I find myself praying in Muslim prayers that is in Arabic and later I notice that I'm praying in a Christian way. I say to myself, "Oh God, I am sure you understand me, you know what I mean." I talk to God just like

He's my friend. I actually did not realise at that point that I had lost my spiritual identity. I did not really think my spirituality mattered.

Upon arriving in Australia, I thought that I could get a job in the IT sector. I had completed my course in Oracle 9i Database Administration and Mastermind Series on Software Engineering (Java Technologies) as my qualifications were recognised almost everywhere. However, I could not find a job in this field. So, I decided to look into the health sector due to its flexibility. Initially, I was an age care worker looking after the elderly in a nursing home after the completion of its required course. I was just like my Dad and mum, it was never enough, we all always wanted to be visible and at the top of our mountains. My family faced a lot of difficulties, but God never left us, God made us even stronger. My dad worked as the Chairman of Odu'a Investment Limited in Nigeria and he enjoyed his printing firm where he did all kinds of desktop publishing work. My mum also worked really hard, she retired as a surveyor after thirty-five years of service from The Ministry of Works and Housing, also in Nigeria. I cannot help it but to be that great person that God has made me to be, I could not hide my communication and interpersonal relationship skills as well as my leadership skills.

After a while, I completed a Certificate IV in Nursing from RMIT University, a Certificate IV in Disability Support Work and a Bachelor of Nursing from the University of South Australia. Even with that I am still looking for ways to and keep improving on myself personally and professionally daily. My mixed spirituality experience was beneficial to my nursing career, I am a lover of life and I love people so my nursing career was just the right profession for my personality. When I worked in the nursing home I liked talking to the residents. I would tell them what I was up to, sang with and sang for the residents and I could see it made them happy. Sometimes, when I arrived at the nursing home I would be told, "So and so is looking for you." Then I would spend extra time with them. I am happy being a nurse. Initially, when I looked back, I usually thought "what a waste to have spent so much money and effort to develop IT skills and not really work with it" But I soon realised that no education is a waste, my extra education did help because in the nursing homes and in the hospitals which I have worked, we use computers for almost every documentation. Studying IT helped me adopt my new career even more. Most of my studies in Australia were completed online, so my IT skills was not a waste after all.

After my nursing education, I enrolled for a graduate nursing program and worked for six months in a palliative care unit where patients mostly died. This also played a role in my thinking perspective about life and death and my spiritual life. On the palliative ward, we encouraged spirituality, accepted and respected the religion and choices of everyone. Due to my Muslim background, I knew the basics of certain rules when a muslin passed away and how to care for a dying Muslim patient. I really enjoyed connecting with my patients and their family. Whenever I went into a Muslim patient's room, I would say in Arabic, 'As-salamu alaykum' (which means peace be unto you), they usually responded well and displayed a sense of trust and rest of mind. When patients connect with you in a way, they want you to do everything for them, and I did, willingly to the best of my ability and as per my code of practice. When I see Catholic patients too, I engage with them also. I tell them that I went to a Catholic school and this starts a conversation. This way I sometimes develop a therapeutic relationship with my patients easily. I noticed that I can easily connect with both Muslims and Christians, I really enjoy nursing and find joy in it.

I remember when I first got to Australia, culturally everything was a surprise. I remember going into Centrelink and an employee asked me, "When did you arrive?" I replied, "Last week," and she said, "Do you speak English?" I said, "Yes, I do." She said you speak it very well too. Honestly, I never knew anyone who didn't speak English. I never met anyone struggling to speak English until I started working and met some others who did. This made me really appreciative that English was spoken in Nigeria. I counted myself as one of the lucky ones because at least I didn't have to go through the process of learning a new language before looking for a job. It was easy for me to communicate with people. The food also shocked me. Everything tasted different – the milk, the bread, the butter, the eggs. My children didn't worry; they were little. But I found it difficult for the first few weeks to eat what I really wanted to. At least now, I now know some African stores that sell a few things even though they are really expensive.

Titilope Alao's family in 2015.

I've always wanted to also see, touch, feel and stand in the snow and watch it fall over me. I was waiting for the snow to fall and was told that snow doesn't fall in certain parts of Melbourne and that one had to go to certain mountains. I said to myself, "What! Are you kidding me? I flew all the way from Nigeria and there is no snow." Up till now I haven't experienced snow because of my son's sickle cell disease condition which I now see as a flimsy excuse.

Generally, I care too much for people almost at the expense of my own peace of mind which people take for granted. I believe that what you give is what you get in abundance and the reward of what I give is not from man but from God. I'm somebody who used to worry a lot, I even worried that I worried a lot. My teacher always said, "You can't always be perfect," but I always wanted everything to be perfect and still work towards perfection which is impossible. I thought I had peace until I had a terrible experience that exposed and stretched my faith. Well, I have now found true peace within myself through Christ Jesus. True Peace of mind is very important. People don't get it until they actually experience that true peace themselves. True peace is understanding oneself spiritually because we are spiritual beings, true peace is satisfaction in what we do, loving oneself and loving others equally. If you appreciate yourself, love yourself and appreciate everything, then you can appreciate another person.

It was in the middle of the year 2016 that I had this terrible experience when I got involved with trying to uplift the spirit of another person. Really, this is what I love doing, to care for people, to inspire and encourage others, to help in any way within my power, I derived so much joy in doing this. I believe that, I was born to do this but I never realised that I was not spiritually fit to do it.

In the process of my genuine support for the vulnerable, I became vulnerable myself because I was not spiritually fit to assist, there was a break in the cycle of love. I know understand the elements of love cycle which includes loving God with all of your heart, loving yourself with the love of God and loving others with the love of God. You see, if there is a break in the love cycle, there will be a problem which is what got me into trouble. I got attacked spiritually.

This was how my adventure with Christ Jesus began. You all know that whenever we have problems, we tend to quickly run to God, which is exactly what I did. I ran to God. I knew it was only God would could save me and my family at that time. That terrible and life changing mistake was not going to stop me from doing good and serving others so I quickly cleaned up my mess, I could either be pitiful or prayerful, so I began to pray. I could not do it alone so I invited Jesus to help me clean my mess because you see, in life if you want to move forward and have progress, you have to leave your past behind you and you don't point fingers at anyone. Soon after rededicating my life to Jesus again, I received the gift of the Holy Spirit, not because I was a nice young lady or because I was a Registered Nurse, it was all for a purpose, it was by the grace and mercy of God Almighty (Eph. 2: 8-9). God had a plan for me.

So I started going to church and bible study. I have always liked to be a good student. Anyways, I always like to follow the rules anywhere I go, whether at work or at school, or in the community so why not in the church. I have always heard it that songs of praise was the highest form of worship, I loved it anyway so that did not bother me at all, so I made sure that I continued my praise and worship, every now and then. I really love to obey God, I suppose God knew me and picked me for this purpose, God knew that I would do anything just to praise and worship him not with my lips and dancing but from the bottom of my heart and with truth. Whenever I heard any new teaching in bible study, I made sure that I obeyed those laws, even when I made a mistake, I tried my best and quickly apologised to God, You see, I really fear God, I would do anything for Him not to be angry at me. One thing I did notice was that even though pastors preached, their actions and the actions of those present in the church contradicted their teachings. It did not take me too long before I moved out of the building called church. Anyways, one day at bible study, we were told to find a suitable time to pray and praise God. To form an altar, so to speak, where you pray and worship God. Why not? Why would I not try my best to do that? The moment I received Sweet Jesus back into my life, I could see the transformation in me and in my home almost immediately, things started to turn around from good to better and almost the best, so I thought to myself, if praying, praising God and worshipping Him will make me and my home happy, I might as well try so hard to make it happen every day. I love my family, so I tried hard like it was an exam. Trust me, there were times where I could feel the presence of the lord while worshipping Him, sometimes it felt like I was in heaven but really I could not see anything but I felt it and believed it, I felt that fullness in my stomach, that deep fullness when the Holy spirit comes upon you, I love it, I love being in that state, I love being in the presence of God.

So I made it a priority to wake up in the middle of the night, you know there were times when I was really tired but I always got a prompt from the Holy spirit to praise and worship, you see God loves it when we honour Him, sometimes it felt like an angel came to remind me of worship time, sometimes I would lean towards the flesh and just sleep while sometimes, I would get up. I felt the need to praise God so much, to show Him my appreciation on how he saved me and my family from calamity and also to shame the devil, so that went on for days. Oh, if I had known, I would have written the date down, even though I sometimes remember the experience, I never thought I could share it. It all began in my son's room, sometimes my son would creep into our room and I would just go to his room to pray instead, I don't usually like disturbing anyone when I am praising my God, I do it with great love and intensity, I worship God anyway and anyhow I like, sometimes, I jump, sometimes I cry, sometimes, I just lay down flat on the ground even though emotions did not determine the purity of the heart. I knew only God could examine and judge the heart. Anyway I began praising God the way I wanted that day and suddenly from praise to praise this song came out of my mouth.

I sang this song over and over again with great intense:

Lord I lift your name on high
Lord I love to sing your praises
I'm so glad you are in my life
I'm so glad you came to save us.
You came from heaven to earth, to show the way
From the earth to the cross, my debt to pay
From the cross to the grave, from the grave to the sky
Lord I lift your name on high.

I did not realise at that time that Jesus was in the room with me, you know, I knew then that he is always present in my heart but I never expected this experience. Suddenly, I was in the spiritual realm, standing there was Jesus, in His white robe, his silky hair, I started caressing his hair back and forth, it was so smooth, then I went ahead and kissed Him on His fore head, YES! I kissed Jesus on his forehead and I loved it, it felt so holy, so I went ahead caressing his hands and legs too, this continued for a while for about five to ten minutes till I was back in my son's room in the physical. I tell you, I felt so full that I could not eat that morning. I was filled with God. The word of God is living and active and if you believe, you will truly experience God (Heb. 4.12).

[That you may really come] to know [practically, [a]through experience for yourselves] the love of Christ, which far surpasses [b]mere knowledge [without experience]; that you may be filled [through all your being] [c]unto all the fullness of God [may have the richest measure of the divine Presence, and [d] become a body wholly filled and flooded with God Himself]! Ephesians 3.19

In the scriptures, "kiss the Son" simply demonstrates your love, intimacy and unity with God, the Father, the Son and the Holy Spirit.

It means to honour God in truth, to worship him with humility, fear and tremble and to show your acceptance and love for Jesus.

In the world we live in today, everybody is working so hard to achieve professionally, to acquire wealth or to live comfortable. God already promised us all of these things you know, he promised to give us every other thing we need if we seek Him first (Matt. 6.33). You see, most people are so full of intellectual ability. I heard this from someone, God knows who, that people nowadays have fat heads and lean souls, don't be led by your head but be led by the Spirit. Remember that if you die, you will take nothing, you will be left with your soul, so while you are struggling with everyday busy life, create time to feed your soul just as you create time to feed your body (3 John 2).

In my years of nursing experience and knowledge gained from nursing experts, it is well known that holistic care is provided considering a person's social, physical, psychological and spiritual state. Why would the healthcare system care about your spiritual state? It is because it matters but unfortunately, spirituality is often left out of the picture until someone is in trouble, sick or ill, that is when people remember God. How about including the growth and development of your spiritual life too while developing personally and professionally?

It is of great importance and an advantage to you to bear good fruits in all areas of your life. Developing spiritually will help you develop in all areas of your life including professionally. This is what God wants for you but is it what you want for yourself? You can only achieve this by walking with God. Everybody knows God or think they know God. What really differentiates one Christian believer from another is his or her personal relationship and fellowship with the Father, Son and the Holy Spirit, which gives a direct access or the hot line to God (Eph. 2.18), which is to the person's benefit (John 16: 7). Fellowship with God means that you are united with the Father, Son and Spirit not just for your purpose but to help disciple the nations, meaning, to love and serve others and to show others how to do the same (Matt. 28:19). You can only form a relationship with God through studying the word of God. Knowing God's words gives you the privilege to have that intimate and permanent relationship with God, the minute we allow Jesus into our lives, when he comes in, he comes in to stay, how much closer do you think you can get? You get the fullness of God Himself. You become to hear from God and do things you never imagined you could ever do, even professionally. When God steps in, He will look after you holistically. The price you pay for your close fellowship with God is your time and genuineness, don't hold back just get soaked in God's love. When you are full of God, the enemy won't be able to stand you, the enemy cannot stand your boldness and confidence in God. You need that confidence in your business too.

So no matter what the circumstances or trouble you may be facing, do not let anything or anyone even your job separates you from the love of God (Rom. 8.35-36), your trouble is not due to the lack of love from God. Know that even when people do not see and understand your personal relationship with God, even when they don't get it, don't worry because they don't have to get it anyway, it is between you and God, , the proof that you are a chosen child of God is that even after all those trouble you come out victorious. In all, you are more than conquerors even in our career, God is always there in the good and bad times, often people seem not to get this. They believe that when you have a trouble you are forsaken, you may be forsaken by man but never forsaken by God, God loves you with your imperfection. Don't be ashamed of your intimacy with God, remember that you are the apple of God's eye (Zech. 2.7-8).

It is time to begin to see with an eye of faith, it is time to start living a life of purpose, do not live based on your emotions, the enemy loves the feeling of insecurity, fear, anger, lack of forgiveness and alike. Being bold and confident not in yourself but in God intimately will scare the enemy away. Ensure that you are rooted deeply in God's love and you will begin to experience God spiritually and physically. You should begin to seek God's presence instead of presents, people often seek the gifts instead of the giver of the gifts, remember that if you have the giver, then you have all the gifts available to you (Ps. 91.1).

In our busy world today, distraction is one of the main things that hinders people from forming a relationship with God. Distractions such as entertainment, work overtime, the demand from people or a people pleasing attitude and especially noise to mention a few. All these things are a distraction and with them going on in your life without balance, you cannot please God or hear from God or even work effectively. This was demonstrated in the scriptures about two sisters, Martha and Mary who received Jesus into their homes, Martha was very busy, so occupied trying to host but her sister Mary seized the opportunity, sat down at Jesus's feet and listened to his preaching (Luke 10:40). What this scripture is trying to say is we need to have a balance in all areas of our life, we cannot just face work or leisure and forget our spiritual life likewise it cannot be all about our spiritual life without work or rest.

The key message here for you and me is to develop our spiritual life. If we develop our spiritual life with Jesus, we will experience and know everything we need to know even about your professional and personal life. Do not be satisfied with, I am just okay, work with excellence, go for the best in life, make sure that when you are climbing the ladder up, you don't make others stumble and don't be a stumbling block to yourself too (phil. 1.10). Don't struggle, let Jesus help you.

Titilope Alao
Ambassador for Christ's Peace

Puff Puff (Deep fried Dough)

Nigerians and Cameroonians call this delicious and easy to make snack Puff-Puff, while the Ghanaians call it Bofrot. It is a quick on the go snack for the family and also good for picnics and birthdays. On several occasions I have made Puff-Puff for my children to take to school on multicultural day events and everyone loved it.

INGREDIENTS

All ingredients can be modified to suit individual tastes.

3 cups self-rising flour
1 tsp quick rise yeast
50g sugar
½ tsp of nutmeg
2 cups lukewarm water
(more or less, until the correct consistency is reached)
Olive oil for frying

METHOD

1. Pour the flour in a big bowl and add all the ingredients.
2. Start adding the lukewarm water slowly till the correct texture is achieved.
3. Mix by hand or using a wooden spoon until there are no lumps.
4. Leave the mixture in a bowl to rise for 50 minutes or more.
5. Pour the olive oil into a deep pan and heat up.
6. Scoop out the dough mixture according to your preferred size and drop into the sizzling oil. Cook one first to test the heat of the oil.
7. Fry until golden brown and place on a serviette. Enjoy.

OUR PACIFIC PROJECTS
WFWP Australia.org

SunHak Primary School
(Solomon Islands)

In 2010, WFWP Japan provided funding for the building of the kindergarten. Since then, WFWP Australia has provided school materials and equipment. Located in the Solomon Islands capital of Honiara, it is situated close to the city centre. The private school is recognised by the government and is growing into a full primary school. With a family centred philosophy of teaching children to develop their sense of community through sharing, developing empathy and understanding for each other, the Academy has the reputation of being the best school in the area.

Pacific Islands Scholarship Fund
(Solomon Islands, Vanuatu)

The WFWP "Pacific Island Scholarship Fund", is a not for profit development program launched in March 2017 that aims to provide young adults from Solomon Islands and Vanuatu with opportunities to access empowering education programs in their own country.

Women's Sewing Centres
(Vanuatu, Samoa, Solomon Islands, PNG)

Our Women's Sewing Centres provide Island women the opportunity to gain skills and support their families economically. With the short term goal to bring women together to learn and/or volunteer their skills, the long-term goal is for women to become economically independent. Our most developed sewing centre is in Honiara in the Solomon Islands and closely collaborates with the SunHak School, providing uniforms and funds.. The sewing centre is currently expanding, as more women join and new projects are developed. Other sewing centres are in Vanuatu, Samoa, Fiji and PNG.

Books for the Islands
(Solomon Islands, Vanuatu, Fiji, Samoa, PNG)

WFWP Australia initiated the 'Book for the Islands Project' in 2008. Since then, we have shipped thousands of boxes of children's books to local primary schools in Vanuatu, the Solomon Islands, Samoa and PNG because many of the Island nation schools do not have libraries. WFWP Australia has worked towards expanding the resources of school libraries by suppling good quality children's books, either in the English or French language.

Find Out More

Endeavour Credit Fund

Endeavour Credit aims to empower women in the Island Nations of Oceania by directly investing in their business idea, through a micro-credit loan. Studies show that when women are given economic opportunity, it benefits not only their families, but their community, and ultimately national economic development. Highlighting the first Global Goal, providing economic opportunities for women puts poverty reduction on a faster track. Recipients are women with low to moderate-income who have viable business ideas and strong business plans that do not meet the criteria of banks or other traditional lenders.

Contact Us

National Office
A: 42-46 Bartley Road, Belgrave Heights VIC 3160
P: (03) 5968 2664

QLD Chapter
A: PO Box 631, Annerley QLD 4103

NSW Chapter
A: 824-826 George St, Chippendale, NSW 2008

WFWP International
W: www.wfwp.org

WFWP Australia
W: www.wfwpaustralia.org
E: contact@wfwpaustralia.org

New Hope Academy Kindergarten and SunHak Primary School

The service component of our mission is to:

Work along side women to build their capability, empower them with the means to enable their children to obtain a formal education, and provide them with the opportunity to be financially stable through sustainable home-based businesses.

With an initial intake of forty students in 2011, NHA commenced through the support of WFWP Japan and WFWP Australia. It has a family centred philosophy of teaching children to develop their sense of community through sharing, developing empathy and having understanding for each other.

In 2018 the Academy developed into a Primary School named SunHak Primary. Even with minimal equipment and playground facilities, it now has the reputation of being the best school in the area.

As the Sun Hak Primary school caters for the increasing number of student enrolments, the school is expanding to a new and larger building in downtown Honiara.

WFWP Australia solar panel donation to NHA (2016)

www.wfwpaustralia.org
contact@wfwpaustralia.org
42-46 Bartley Rd, Belgrave Heights 3160

Women's Federation for World Peace Australia

The Oceania region of the Women's Federation for World Peace International has a footprint in Australia, New Zealand, Solomon Islands, Vanuatu, PNG, Samoa and Fiji. WFWP International was inaugurated in 1992 and is active in 122 nations.

Empowering Women | Strengthening Families | Connecting Communities

Find Out More